Southampton
Gateway to England

TERRACE

Southampton
Gateway to England

Jan and Peter Boyd-Smith

RED POST

For Simon and Anna

We received so much positive feedback from our first book, *Southampton in Focus* on which we worked together in 1996, that we decided to produce another book along similer lines.

Southampton: Gateway to England is a new selection from our extensive collection of old postcards and photographs of Southampton and covers the period from the 1880s to the 1960s. In response to requests from many of our readers we have expanded the sections on Southampton's docks and *RMS Titanic*.

Unless otherwise captioned, all items are, or were, the property of the authors. Many of the pictures featured in this book were produced by companies that no longer exist or we have been unable to trace. If we have inadvertently infringed anyone's rights, we hope they will excuse us.

We hope you enjoy reading this book as much as we enjoyed writing it.

Jan and Peter Boyd-Smith
Southampton October 2002

First published in 2002 by Red Post Books

Designed and produced by Crispin Goodall
Printed and bound by The Cromwell Press

A CIP catalogue record for this book is available from the British Library.

ISBN 1-901533-07-6

Red Post Books
81 Saxonhurst Road
Bournemouth
Dorset
BH10 6JF

Telephone: +44 (0) 1202 511517
Fax: +44 (0) 1202 387912

Red Post Books publish illustrated non-fiction books. If you have a title which you think may be of interest, we would be pleased to hear from you. Address your enquiry to the Editorial Director at the above address.

Contents

Introduction

Southampton's unusual double tide and her sheltered position in the lee of the Isle of Wight made her a natural port. The port's location together with the opening of the docks and the town's accessibility by train to all parts of the country ensured the rapid expansion of the town. In 1838 the foundation stone for the docks was laid although construction was not completed until 1842. The arrival of the railway in 1840 with a fast and reliable line to London followed by lines to Dorchester and Salisbury made access to all parts of the country possible. For more than 150 years the docks have witnessed the loading and unloading of freight, the arrival and departure of passengers and their luggage and embarking and disembarking of troops in times of war. The importance of Southampton as a port resulted in the town often being referred to over the years as the 'gateway to England', the 'gateway to Britain' or even the 'gateway to the Empire'.

By the middle of the 19th century Southampton was ranked as the fifth most important port in Britain. It was at this time that the Royal Mail Steam Packet Co and the Peninsular and Oriental Steam Packet Company began their long association with the port. In 1861, the Isle of Wight and South of England Royal Mail Steam Packet Company was formed. This local company operated paddle-steamers and a service continues today between the Island and the mainland with Red Funnel. The ever-increasing size of ships resulted in the need to build more quays, docks and drydocks, the largest of which was the Empress Dock, opened in 1890 by Queen Victoria.

During the 1840s iron foundries and shipbuilding yards sprang up along the banks of the River Itchen at Northam. The best known of these was Day Summers, which continued in business until 1928. All around these yards streets of small terraced houses were being built, partly on reclaimed marshland, to house the ever growing workforce of the shipyards and the docks. In the town centre the architecture was a pleasing mixture of genteel Georgian and imposing Victorian buildings standing next to one another. Unfortunately the heavy bomb damage during the Blitz of the Second World War resulted in the destruction of most of these lovely old buildings. Above Bar Street and High Street were thriving thoroughfares and the number of shops in the town had begun to increase to cater for the growing population. The first department stores came to Southampton in the late 1850s. In 1860 Edwin Jones opened a small shop in East Street which grew to become the largest department store in town. Edwin Jones and Co Limited continued to trade at Queen's Buildings until the store was bought out by Debenhams. E Mayes and Son opened in 1870 and later became Owen Owens; Plummer Roddis and Tyrell and Green opened in the 1890s.

By the beginning of the 20th century Southampton had already established itself as Britain's premier port. When White Star and Cunard Lines moved from Liverpool to Southampton in 1907 and 1919 respectively, the town was also recognised as the largest passenger port in Britain. Just a few short years into the new century saw Southampton rocked by a tragedy that is still keenly felt. At midnight on April 3, 1912, *RMS Titanic*, the world's largest ship, arrived at Southampton. She was huge – at 46,000 tons, the largest moving object built by man. For the next week she took on stores and cargo as workmen added the finishing touches to her fabulous interior. During the week that she was berthed at the White Star dock she also embarked her crew. Most were from Southampton and as there was a docks strike in Britain at that time, a berth on this modern leviathan was extremely sought after. At noon on a cold Wednesday April 10, she cast off her ropes and departed on her maiden voyage to Cherbourg, Queenstown and New York. A small crowd gathered to watch her sail: after all, she was just another ship, larger than others and brand new, but her sister *RMS Olympic* had been using the port for nearly a year and she was the one that had attracted the large crowds. As she left Ocean Dock she turned into the Test and passing 38 berth (now the *QEII* terminal) her suction caused ropes to break on the American liner *New York* which began to swing out and almost collide with *Titanic*. Only superb seamanship on board the tug Vulcan, together with the expertise of Pilot Bowyer and *Titanic's* Captain Smith, averted a collision and she continued her voyage into history. She arrived at Cherbourg in the evening and sailed for Queenstown in Ireland that same night, arriving the following day. After picking up her final passengers she set sail for the final leg of her journey at 1.30pm on April 11.

The voyage was uneventful until the night of Sunday April 14. Dinner had been served and most passengers had retired to their staterooms or cabins for the night. At 11.40pm while steaming at 21 knots she collided with an iceberg. Within minutes it was obvious to Captain Smith and the ship's designer, Thomas Andrews, that the ship was going to sink. There were 2,205 passengers and crew on board and insufficient lifeboats for all; 705 people were rescued and 1,500 did not survive. The devastating loss of life greatly affected the town; 549 of the crew members that were lost were from Southampton. The families of Chapel and Northam were particularly devastated as most of the crew lived in homes in the many terraced streets that formed a very closely knit community. This was, and still is, the worst peacetime tragedy to hit any British town.

Within two years of the Titanic tragedy was the start of the 'Great War', 1914-18. The local people became accustomed to seeing not only their own brave men enlisting, but thousands of men from across the country marching through the Bargate to sail in troopships bound for France or the Dardanelles. Many would never return, while others would find themselves recovering at the huge military hospital at Netley. Sadly many of those did not recover and are buried in the peaceful cemetery in the hospital grounds which are now the Royal Victoria Country Park. Across the years Southampton has been a port of departure or return for the British military. During the 19th century these included battalions bound for the Crimean, Zulu and Boer Wars. In the last century thousands of troops heading off to fight in the battles of the First and Second World Wars and the Korean and Falklands Wars often saw their last glimpse of England as they sailed down Southampton Water.

By the turn of the 20th century the villages of Shirley, Bitterne and Swaythling were slowly being swallowed up by the expansion of Southampton. The late 1880s saw Shirley especially becoming a large built up area with streets of terraced houses standing alongside avenues of more imposing detached villas. With the extension of the tram routes in the early 1900s the new suburbs of Bitterne Manor and Bitterne Park on the east of the River Itchen grew rapidly. Woolston remained a village until the 1890s but following the purchase of the old Fays shipbuilding yard in 1902 by John I Thorneycroft, its population mushroomed. The 1930s saw the development of social housing at Coxford, Swaythling and Merry Oak while the 1950s, 1960s and 1970s saw further expansion of the suburbs. New estates were built on the east of the river at Harefield, Thornhill and Weston and on the west side at Millbrook and Lordshill. From the 1920s to the 1950s the port was in its heyday; 1936 was the year that the Cunarder *RMS Queen Mary* sailed on her maiden voyage from

Southampton to New York. She was the most popular liner that used the port and on her last voyage to Long Beach in California in 1967, an estimated 50,000 people watched her sail.

The local townspeople together with those from the surrounding area could choose from a wide range of entertainment. The Royal Pier had frequent band concerts and shows. Theatres, including the Grand, the Empire and the Hippodrome, produced live shows while moving pictures were particularly popular with Sotonians. In 1940 Southampton had no less than fourteen cinemas in the town centre and the suburbs, offering a wide choice of films that usually were changed twice weekly. Sports fans had use of the Sports Centre, which opened in the 1930s with a purpose built cycle track. There was speedway and greyhound racing at the Stadium at Bannister Park. Swimmers could use the public baths and the Lido. Keen football fans could watch Saints play at the Dell while cricket supporters could watch Hampshire play at the County Ground. Both teams have recently been re-located to the new St Mary's Stadium at Northam and the Rose Bowl at West End on the outskirts of the city.

On September 3, 1939, war was declared and the town suffered hard during the following six years, especially in the Blitz. The air raids of November 30 and December 1, 1940, saw the virtual destruction of both Above Bar Street and High Street. While 1,169 properties were damaged or completely destroyed, 137 people lost their lives. In June 1944 every river, dock and estuary around Southampton was packed with landing craft and ships as the Allied invasion of France got underway.

After the devastation of the town during the war, a period of rejuvenation took place with extensive building programmes. While a Royal Charter awarded Southampton University full university status in April 1952, it was not until 1964 that the town finally became the city of Southampton. During the 1950s and 1960s passenger liners were kept busy carrying emigrants to new lives in Canada, Australia, New Zealand and South Africa.

In recent years there have been major changes to the city centre. The modern trend for shopping has resulted in the creation of Marlands, Bargate and West Quay shopping malls. The West Quay development has encouraged many of the established stores to move there including Marks and Spencer and Tyrell and Green (now John Lewis) who have become anchor stores. Historically the commercial centre of Southampton has shifted westwards from Saxon times at Hamwic in Chapel and St Marys, to medieval Southampton within the town walls and now on to the West Quay development.

ED. JACKSON
MILL & SONS
STEAM DYERS

CHAPTER ONE
TOWN CENTRE

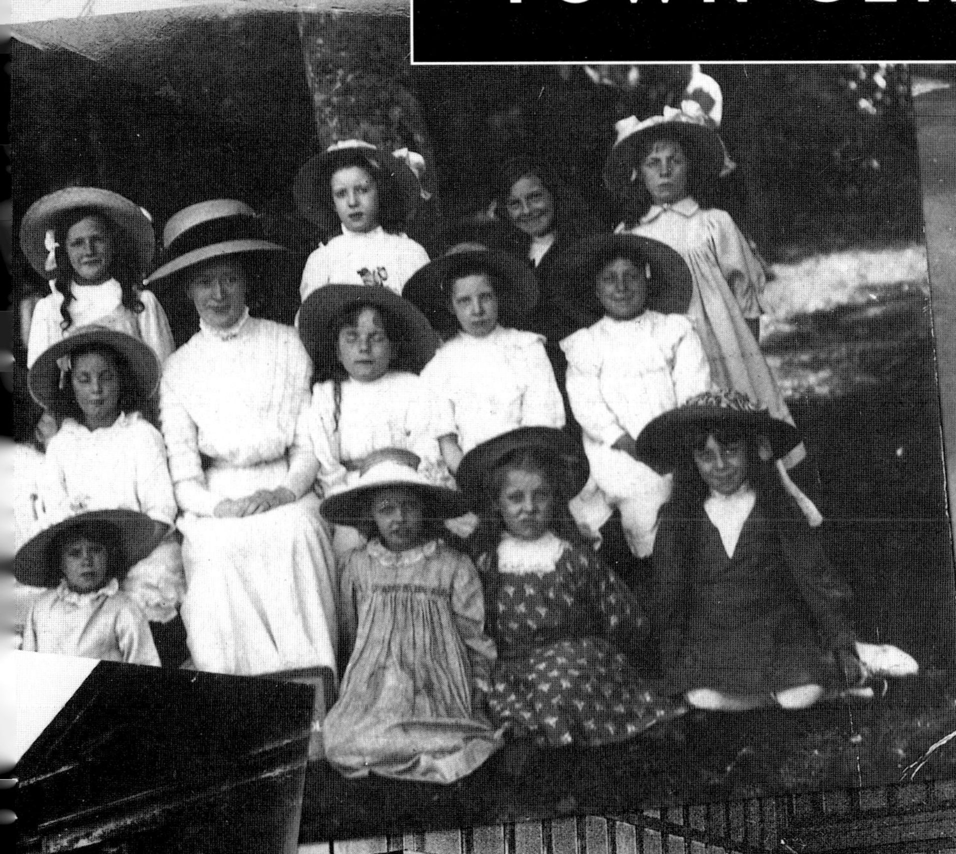

TOP: This view of Above Bar and the Bargate was taken very early in the morning in the early 1900s. At the Above Bar Coffee Tavern, dinner is advertised at 6d (2.5p) and coffee and chocolate at 1d (0.5p) a cup. Next door is Southampton's circulating library.

ABOVE: Below Bar in the 1890s. In the foreground is All Saints Church that stood at the corner of East Street. Richard Allen the chocolate maker is on the left side of the picture. The horse-drawn tram is advertising Mill and Sons, Steam Dyers. George Jackson's, on the left, sold groceries and patent medicines.

TOP: The High Street in the 1890s, unlike today, was a bustling thoroughfare. The spire of Holyrood church is on the right with All Saints in the distance. Next to the tram two men are busy painting the tram pole. The Inland Revenue office is on the left opposite the Continental Café and Restaurant. In the right foreground is the lamp belonging to the Post Office which is just out of shot. This remained as the headquarters and main Post Office until a few years ago. Most of the other buildings were destroyed in the bombing during the Second World War.

ABOVE: Pembroke Square at the Bargate in 1905. This was a pretty little cul-de-sac with small shops, demolished in 1933 to make way for the road around the Bargate. The enamel sign on the railings is a recruiting notice for the King's Army. The man with the white cap had responsibility for controlling the traffic going through the Bargate's central arch.

ABOVE: The old Police Station next to the Bargate at the turn of the century. In the 1930s the inclusion of purpose built facilities at the new Civic Centre resulted in the closing of this old station.

OPPOSITE ABOVE: The top of the High Street in the early 1930s. On the right are the District Offices of the Liverpool and London and Globe Insurance Company. Next door is Henry Chard the gentlemen's outfitter. These buildings would not be there much longer, as all of this block was later demolished to enable traffic to go round the Bargate. Traffic going through the Bargate had reached such a peak that it had been necessary to erect traffic lights which can be seen in between the two arches on the left of the picture.

OPPOSITE: The forerunner of the University of Southampton was situated in the High Street. Henry Robinson Hartley bequeathed to the council, for educational use, a substantial sum of money, his house, works of art and scientific specimens. Together with the acquisition of the two houses next door, the Hartley Institute was created and opened by Lord Palmerston in 1862. Later it became Hartley College and then a University College with degrees awarded from the University of London. The growing popularity for courses saw expansion of student numbers and a re-location to the present site at Highfield in 1914. Full university status was awarded by Royal Charter on April 29, 1952, with the Duke of Wellington as the first Chancellor. The year 2002 marks the university's Golden Jubilee with a number of events being held in celebration. The statues that can be seen on the façade of the building have recently been installed in a peaceful area outside the Hartley Library in University Road This photograph was taken around 1927 when the building was up for sale.

GLOBE INSURANCE Co
LTD.
DISTRICT OFFICE
HENRY CHA
ESTABLISHED
60
YEARS.
SHIRT &
NECKWEAR
SPECIALIST
OUTFITTER.
HENRY CHARD

THIS COMMANDING FREEHOLD PROPERTY
TO BE SOLD
Apply to the Authorised PRINCIPAL LOCAL AGENTS.
FOR SALE
FOR SALE

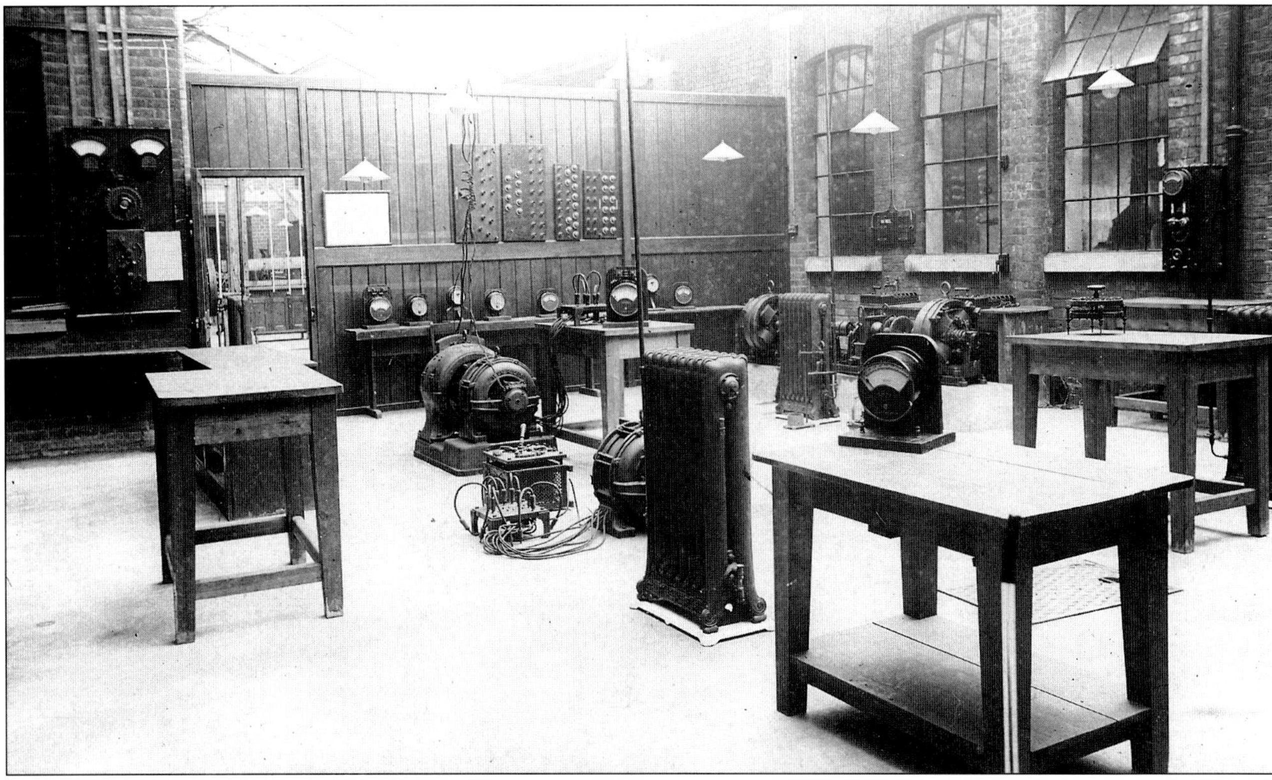

TOP: Inside the old building. A machine shop with work benches and engineering apparatus.

ABOVE: The Dolphin Hotel in High Street around 1900. Built in the 15th century, this building has had an interesting history, first as a public house and then in 1628 as a court. In 1795 the Prince of Wales stayed here and later it became a coaching inn with coaches entering through the central arch. Today its appearance has little changed, except that cars now park in the courtyard where stagecoaches once stood.

TOP: A rooftop view of the High Street looking south in the 1920s. The spire of Holyrood Church is in the centre with an open-top tram about to turn into Bernard Street. In the distance is the huge floating crane with *RMS Majestic* and *RMS Olympic* in the White Star dock, which was also called the Ocean Dock.

ABOVE: Tudor House in Bugle Street as it looked in the 1920s. Originally named Old Palace House and divided into three sections, it became a museum in 1912. In the 1850s the middle section was occupied by a Southampton architect, Mr J George Poole, and his family of twenty-one children. Mr Poole designed the fountain that stood on Asylum Green and the railings around St Mary's Church.

ABOVE: Westgate with views of the sea and Western Esplanade through the archway. Built in the 14th century, this was one of the main gates through the walls into the town. In 1900, when this photograph was taken, the area was a maze of small streets with slum dwellings which were subsequently cleared by the 1920s.

TOP: The Old Tower Inn at 22 Bargate Street. Built in the shadow of the medieval Arundel Tower, the inn traded originally as the Plumbers Arms when it was built in the 1850s. The building was demolished in 1899 and a new building erected. The replacement was then bombed during the Second World War, repaired and finally demolished in the mid-1960s.

ABOVE: The Old Walls and Western Shore at the turn of the century. In the foreground, gathered to watch the photographer at work, the ladies and their children are dressed in fresh bright summer finery in contrast to the poorer children, two of whom are barefoot. The sea came up to the walls until the land was reclaimed in the 1920s.

TOP: The Old Town Walls. Partly built in the 1300s, today they still look much as they did in this early 1900s photograph. The children in this picture may not have seen a photographer before and would have had to keep perfectly still while the photo was taken.

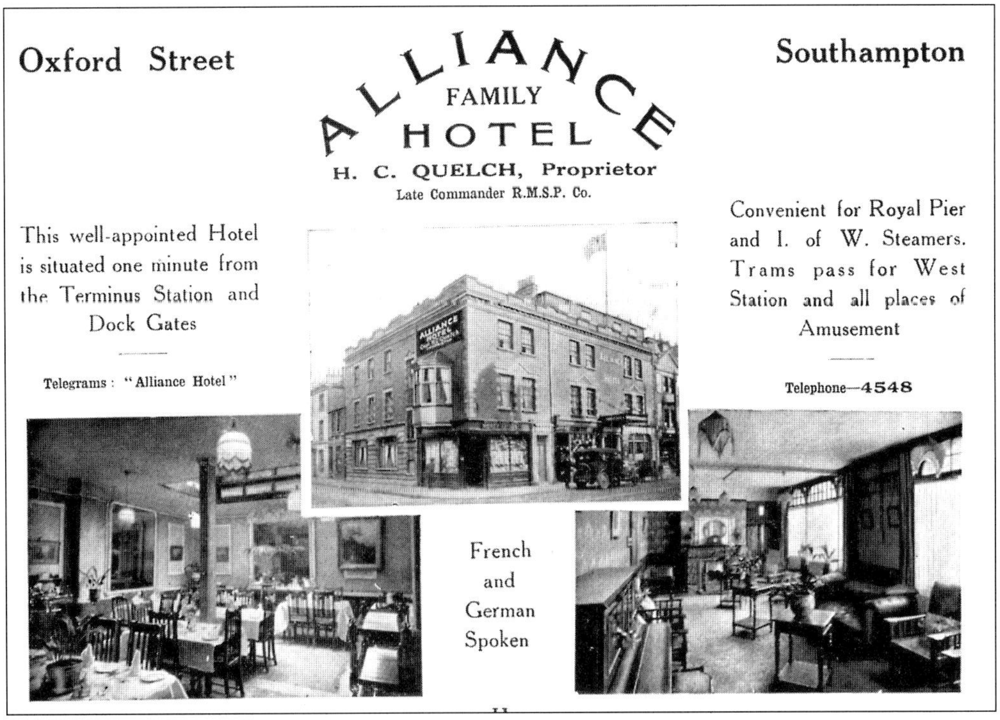

TOP: Western Esplanade around 1900. The cannons were captured during the Crimean War and vanished during a metal drive in the Second World War. The Stella Memorial is to the memory of Mrs Rogers, a brave stewardess aboard *SS Stella*, which was wrecked near the Channel Islands in 1899, with great loss of life.

TOP: The South Western Hotel circa 1905. Originally built as the Imperial Hotel in 1868 but renamed the South Western in 1870, this building has beautifully painted ceilings and a grand marble staircase. J Bruce Ismay, the Chairman of White Star Line, and *Titanic's* designer Thomas Andrews stayed here when the famous liner was in port. The hotel was built with the centre of an open design which allowed easy access for guests arriving or departing at Terminus Station, just behind the hotel. On the right of the picture you can see a train making its way down Canute Road. After the closure of the hotel it was converted to offices for the Cunard Shipping Line.

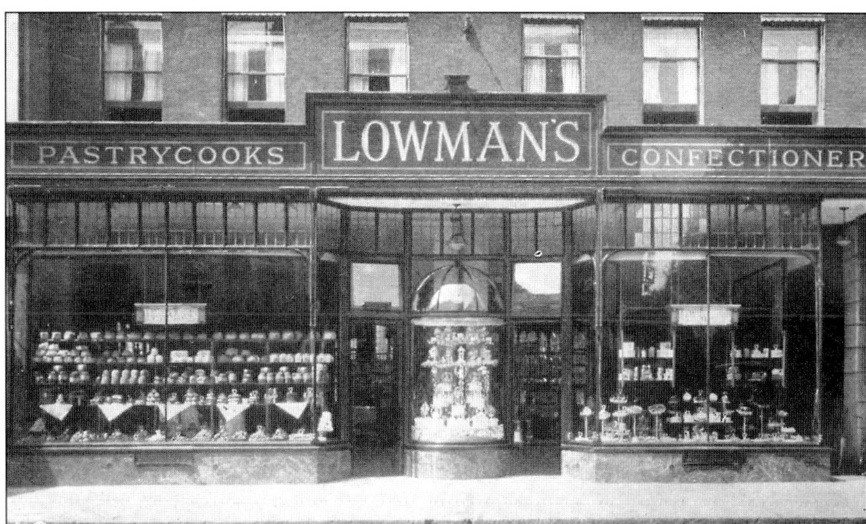

LOWMAN'S CAFE, 91 and 93 ABOVE BAR TEL. 3822
for LUNCHEONS and TEAS
Accommodation for parties visiting Southampton
Head Office, 78/84 PORTSWOOD RD., SOUTHAMPTON TEL. 74061

TOP: The Clock Tower at the junction of New Road and Above Bar Street is pictured early one morning without a soul in sight. Donated to the town in 1889, it incorporated a drinking fountain and horse trough. Due to traffic congestion, the clock was moved in 1934 to its current home at Bitterne Park Triangle. In the right hand corner of the picture is the entrance to the Grand Theatre.

TOP: The girls and their teacher from Above Bar Church grouped together for a photograph to commemorate their Sunday School excursion to Lyndhurst by horse and cart in 1900. The church stood at the corner of Above Bar Street and Ogle Road.

ABOVE: Watts Park on a warm sunny day in Edwardian Southampton. The statue of Isaac Watts was the work of local sculptor R C Lucas and was erected in 1861. This area has changed little and apart from the fashion, this scene is still played out when the sun shines.

TYRRELL & GREEN LTD

This Establishment is now under one management (the same goods at the same prices) with John Lewis & Co. Ltd., of Oxford Street, and Peter Jones, of Sloane Square, London, and other Companies belonging likewise to the John Lewis Partnership

This has no connection with Messrs. Lewis Ltd. of Liverpool and elsewhere

COMPLETE LADIES', MEN'S AND CHILDREN'S OUTFITTERS
SOFT FURNISHING CARPETS AND LINOLEUM
HOUSEHOLD LINENS CHINA AND GLASS IRONMONGERY
A COMPLETE RANGE OF JOHN LEWIS FABRICS ALWAYS IN STOCK

Hairdressing Salons——Ladies', Men's and Children's
Permanent Waving——Macdonald and Eugene Process
Manicure—Certified Chiropodist—Tel. Southampton 4211

A.A. and R.A.C. APPOINTED **BAROVA RESTAURANT** LICENSED

MORNING COFFEE LUNCHEONS TEAS AND DINNERS
TABLE D'HOTE OR A LA CARTE ORCHESTRA
TELEPHONE: SOUTHAMPTON 264011

ABOVE BAR = = = SOUTHAMPTON

TOP: Tramway Junction was where Above Bar Street and Commercial Road met. Tyrell and Green, then on the right side of the photograph later moved to the other side of the road and the Plummer Roddis department store took over the building. Further down the road you can see the Old Clock tower. The open-top tram is packed with people in their summer attire. Tyrell and Green opened in the town in 1897 and moved from Above Bar to the new West Quay centre in 2000 and their name was changed to the John Lewis Partnership.

TOP: Above Bar Street in the 1950s. On the left is the Plummer Roddis Store and opposite is the Gas Board shop. These temporary buildings after the bombing of the 1940s were eventually replaced with permanent and much larger properties. Further up on the right is Swears and Wells the furriers.

ABOVE: Sussex Place, looking south along Above Bar Street at the beginning of the 20th century. On the left is Debenham and Smith the photographers and on the right C E Godfrey and Company's music warehouse. Further along on the right is the Church of Christ and the Philharmonic Hall.

TOP: Cumberland Place overlooking West Park in the 1890s. Today the elegant Regency houses are hotels and offices.

TOP: The Polygon Hotel was originally built in 1768 and was rebuilt in the early 1900s. This photograph shows the hotel in 1934. This establishment was advertised as a high class boarding house and residential hotel with eighty rooms with hot and cold running water, central heating and only $1\frac{1}{2}$ minutes from the Empire Theatre. Within the grounds were croquet lawns and tennis courts.

ABOVE: The proposed design for a new Polygon Hotel that included a theatre. This plan was not implemented, perhaps because the war intervened.

CHANDLERS, HIGH CLASS PHOTOGRAPHERS

(S. A. CHANDLER (SOUTHAMPTON) LTD.) For many years established at 132 Above Bar, Southampton

11 COMMERCIAL ROAD, SOUTHAMPTON—OPPOSITE EMPIRE THEATRE

TELEPHONE: SOUTHAMPTON 2428 Also at Exeter

HIGH CLASS STUDIO PORTRAITURE . COMMERCIAL PHOTOGRAPHY

SOUTHAMPTON'S LEADING HOUSE FOR ALL KODAK SUPPLIES

ABOVE: St Peter's Church in Commercial Road was built in 1846 at a cost of £3,600. This Victorian photograph shows the building surrounded by large grounds. Today it is a bar and restaurant and the grounds have long gone.

TOP: St Winifred's Kindergarten and High School in London Road around 1905. St Paul's Church is top left of the picture.

ABOVE: A view of the old library at the Roman Catholic Training College in The Avenue. Originally opened in 1881 as a school for day pupils and boarders it was considered a 'superior school for young ladies'. Run by the sisters of the La Sainte Union it expanded on September 15, 1904, and took in the first group of sixty female students to commence training as elementary school teachers. The Reverend Mother Antonia was a founder and became the first principal of the college, which is now incorporated into the University of Southampton as New College.

TOP: The training college had peaceful gardens for the students to enjoy. This picture is of the tennis lawn.

ABOVE: St Mary's Street looking towards Northam Road. E Hart & Co is opposite the Kingsland Tavern which is still in business today. Upstairs next door is Hercules Private School for Physical Culture.

J. HARVEY

(LATE W. SUMMERS),

WHOLESALE AND RETAIL

PICTURE FRAME MANUFACTURER

ESTABLISHED 1860.

66, ST. MARY STREET

SOUTHAMPTON.

And 7, STRAND.

Importer of Washable Gilt Mouldings, Window Glass, &c.

Old Picture Frames Re-gilt and made equal to new.

MOUNTS CUT TO ORDER.

OIL PAINTINGS CLEANED, BACK-LINED AND RESTORED.

TOP: St Mary's Street before the First World War looking in the opposite direction. On the right hand side is the entrance to the Workhouse, now City College. This road was a busy shopping area servicing the families that lived in the surrounding streets of St Mary's, Chapel and Northam.

ABOVE: The arrival of the new bells for St Mary's Church by horse and cart was a great occasion for the town. In June 1914, a month after this picture was taken, a pageant was held over a period of ten days. On the last day the bells were rung for the first time. Their sound was to inspire the song *The Bells of St. Mary's*, made famous by Bing Crosby.

ABOVE: St Mary's Church in the street that bears its name. There has been a church on this site since Saxon times but the present church was built in the 1880s. Originally squat with no spire, funds were raised to build an impressive spire that could be seen from far and wide. This picture was taken in 1913 while building work was being carried out.

OPPOSITE: St Mary's in all her glory, with her new spire that looked as though it had always been there.

DOWNEY
FOSTER

TOP: The ancient Crosshouse in Chapel. Originally without a roof this building is believed to date back to medieval times and was built to provide shelter from the wind for passengers waiting to cross the River Itchen by ferryboat.

ABOVE: Northam Road before the trams. This road is the main route into the town from the east and this view today is little changed from how it looked in the early 1900s. The Glebe public house was built in the 1870s and is still in business today as the King Alfred.

TOP: On the opposite side of the road to the Glebe pub before the Second World War, at 76 Northam Road, was Mr Hillier's record shop. He also had an antique shop in St Mary's Road until the 1960s. His son Mick continued in the antiques trade with a shop in Adelaide Road and later St Mary's Street until he died a few years ago. Now his son Tom deals in antiques and books in Northam Road. Three generations of the Hillier family had businesses in the area for almost a century. In the 1950s number 76 became the famous antique shop Bygones, with many regular film star customers who travelled on the 'Queens'.

ABOVE: Further down Northam Road at number 21 in the 1920s, Brophy the picture framers advertised Christmas annuals. Number 25 was Butlers the photographer and gramophone dealer, next door was Fortescue the cycle engineers. Both sold and repaired bicycles. A cycle shop remained in Northam Road until the late 1970s.

Re JOHN ASLATT. Deceased, and Others.

To INVESTORS, SPECULATORS, & BUILDERS.

THOS. MIELL JUNR.

Has received Instructions from the Trustees and Others, to submit to PUBLIC AUCTION, at the

Sale Rooms, Hanover Buildings,

SOUTHAMPTON,

On THURSDAY EVENING, OCTOBER 10th, 1895,

At SEVEN o'clock,

THE FOLLOWING ELIGIBLE

PROPERTIES AND LAND

No. 18, ALBERT STREET, CHAPEL,

FREEHOLD.

Nos. 28, 30, AND 32, BUGLE STREET.

1 to 5, CORONATION TERRACE, St. MARY STREET,

LEASEHOLD.

BUILDING ESTATE, BITTERNE,

FREEHOLD.

CAPITAL FREEHOLD SHOP AND DWELLING-HOUSE,

No. 18, Commercial Road. Southampton.

FREEHOLD LAND, PORTSWOOD ROAD.

Total Rental Value—

PER £173 10S. 0D. ANN.

Solicitors—Messrs. PEARCE & KEELE, 2 St. Michael's Street, and Messrs. GREEN, MOBERLY & GREEN, 10, Portland Terrace.

OPPOSITE: This 1895 advertisement announces the forthcoming auction of properties and land in Chapel, Bugle Street, St Mary's Street and Bitterne. Lot No 3 was 1 to 5 Coronation Terrace, St Mary's Street. Built in 1836, they sold as a single lot in 1895 for £525.

ABOVE: The sender of this charming postcard writes to friends in Bournemouth imagining that they may well, one day, move to Southampton.

174. E. MAYES & SON LTD 174.

W. COX. Confectioner 45
W. COX. CONFECTIONER

'ROVER' CARS
LIMITED

CHAPTER TWO
TRADE AND COMMERCE

TOP: The Criterion Garage in St Mary's Road was one of the few agents in the town for Rover cars. They also had a showroom in London Road. This photograph was taken around 1930. Inside the garage is a car with the registration number TR 7835 – a collector's piece today.

ABOVE: F Baker and Sons had their department store at 55-59 Northam Road, just opposite Northam railway station. The store not only allowed customers to purchase goods on credit but awarded good customers with bonus payouts.

TOP: Further along Northam Road at number 182 stood the Wonder Inn, named after a Southampton-based Channel Islands paddle steamer. The building was demolished in 1960.

ABOVE: This advertising card for A Jones of 33 London Road announces the commencement of their Grand Sale of hand-made evening and promenade shoes.

TOP: On January 3, 1912, Harts Domestic Bazaar in Bridge Street caught fire and was almost totally destroyed. The damage to the bazaar and neighbouring buildings totalled £25,000.

ABOVE: This rare photograph shows some of the firemen having a well deserved break after fighting the fire.

ABOVE: Dewhurst the butchers had a shop at 190 Above Bar Street and sold sausages at 5d (2p) per pound, rabbits at 8d (3p) and steak from 1s (5p) per pound.

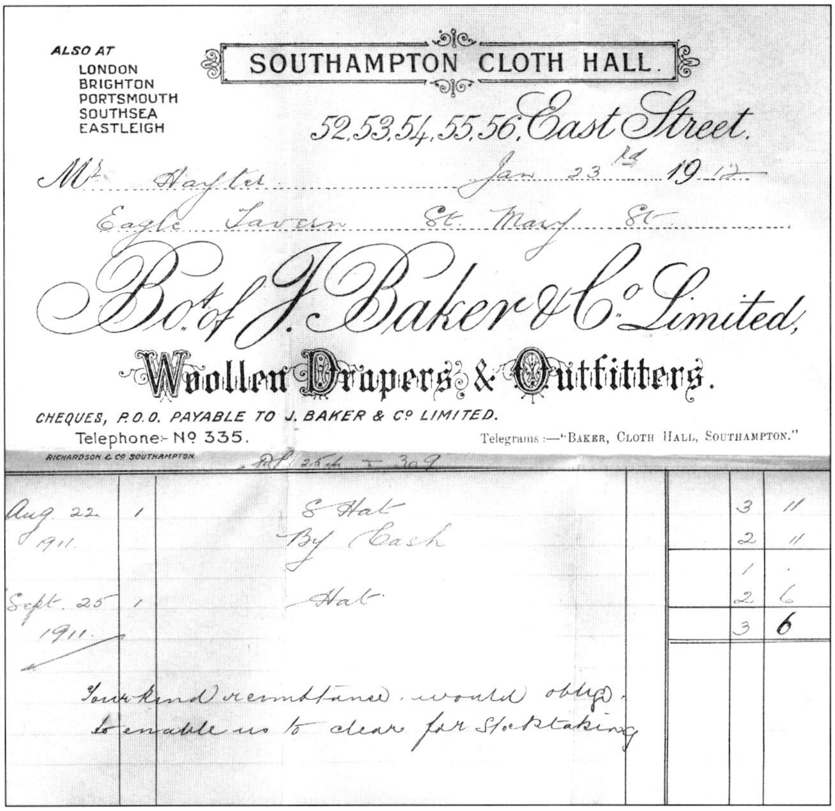

ALSO AT
LONDON
BRIGHTON
PORTSMOUTH
SOUTHSEA
EASTLEIGH

SOUTHAMPTON CLOTH HALL.

52, 53, 54, 55, 56, East Street.

Mr Hayter Jan 23rd 1912
Eagle Tavern St Mary St

Bot. of J. Baker & Co. Limited,
Woollen Drapers & Outfitters.

CHEQUES, P.O.O. PAYABLE TO J. BAKER & Co LIMITED.
Telephone:- No 335.
Telegrams:—"BAKER, CLOTH HALL, SOUTHAMPTON."
RICHARDSON & Co SOUTHAMPTON

Aug 22 1911	1	S Hat	3	11
		By Cash	2	11
			1	.
Sept. 25 1911	1	Hat	2	6
			3	6

Your kind remittance would oblige, to enable us to clear for Stocktaking

RIGHT: A 1912 invoice for J Baker and Company, drapers and outfitters, of East Street. The bill was addressed to Mr Hayter of the Eagle Tavern in St Mary's Street who obviously had a liking for hats – he bought two within a month.

45 W. COX. Confectioner. 45
BOURNVILLE BISCUITS
ROWNTREE'S CLEAR GUMS
CADBURY'S
CHOCOLAT EPPS
ICES

RIGHT: Ward's Restaurant and Refreshment Rooms at 104 High Street. The proprietor Peter Derham specialised in Barlow's genuine ales and stouts. Next door at 105 is Raymond Brown the stationer.

OPPOSITE: W Cox of 45 High Street was a family run confectionery business. Mrs Cox and her assistant have posed for the photograph next to the enticing display of chocolates and sweets in the window.

RIGHT: A 1911 advertising card for The Southampton Gaslight and Coke Company. They had offices in Ogle Road and Above Bar Street with their main works in Marine Parade.

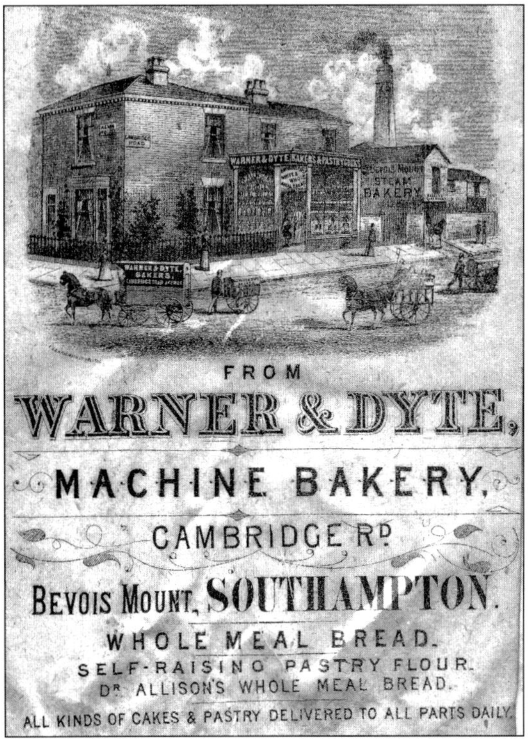

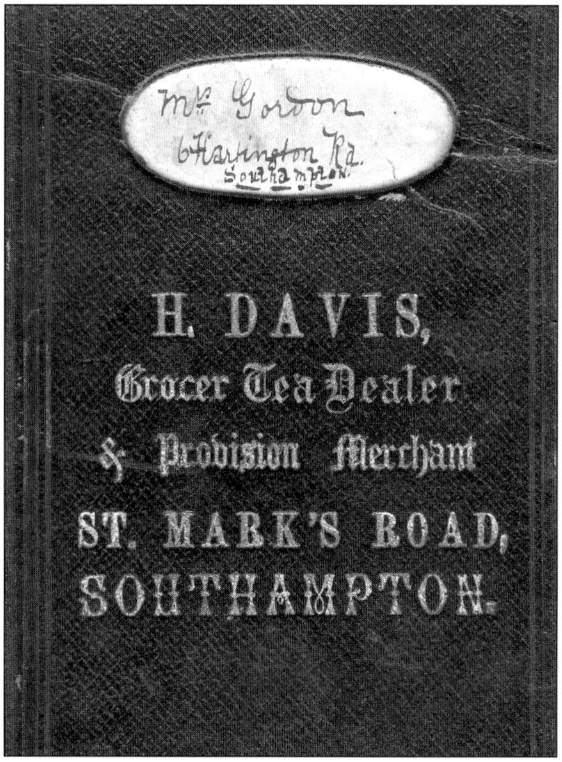

TOP: Mayes and Son of 174 High Street is fondly remembered by many of Southampton's residents. Starting from one small shop, Mayes expanded to become one of the largest and most popular department stores in Southampton. Due to bomb damage in the Second World War a larger store was built. The store became part of the Owen Owen Group, but was closed in the 1990s. The site is now occupied by Argos and T K Maxx. This photograph was taken around 1920.

ABOVE LEFT: A paper bag from Warner and Dyte the bakers of Cambridge Road, Bevois Mount, shows their shop with the steam bakery in the background. A range of bread, cakes and pastries were delivered daily by horse-drawn van or handcart.

OPPOSITE BOTTOM RIGHT: A 1900 account book for H Davis, the grocer and provision merchant of St Mark's Road, in the name of Mrs Gordon of Hartington Road shows half-a-pound of butter cost 7d (3p), a tablet of Sunlight soap 2½d (1p), a lettuce 1d (0.5p) but a cabbage was 3d (1p). Often housewives and housekeepers kept an account at the local grocers and purchases were meticulously recorded on every visit. Grocers had to wait for accounts to be paid, many were not good payers, unlike Mrs Gordon who settled her account regularly.

ABOVE: A catalogue for the Birmingham and Coventry Cycle Company at 149-151 Above Bar Street. Apart from prams and wirelesses, furniture and clothes were also sold. Triumph Motorcycles sold at £24 17s 6d (£24.88). For those wanting a new bicycle, easy terms were offered – 2s 6d (12.5p) deposit and weekly payments of only 1s 6d (7.5p) – but not on a Wednesday afternoon, this was early closing day.

EDWIN JONES & Co. Ld
T J BOND

MECCANO TOYS OF QUALITY
MECCANO
HORNBY-DUBLO
DINKY TOYS
HORNBY TRAINS
Edwin Jones & Co. Ltd
Queens Buildings
SOUTHAMPTON
Tel. 23888
4d
U.K.

OPPOSITE TOP: Edwin Jones' department store as it was in 1933. Built in the 1880s, this store was the result of the foresight of a merchant from Romsey. In the 1870s Edwin Jones had a small shop in East Street. Business was good and he expanded into other shops. After demolishing cottages facing Queens Park, this store was built and modernised in 1933. Sadly this lovely old shop was destroyed during the bombing of 1940. Re-building after the war resulted in the current Queen's Buildings, now owned by the Debenhams Group.

OPPOSITE BELOW: A Meccano catalogue from Edwin Jones in 1956. A boy's delight, this catalogue also covered all the Dinky toys and trains, as the author well remembers.

ABOVE: The Park and East Street entrances of Edwin Jones, in 1933. Alterations took nearly six years.

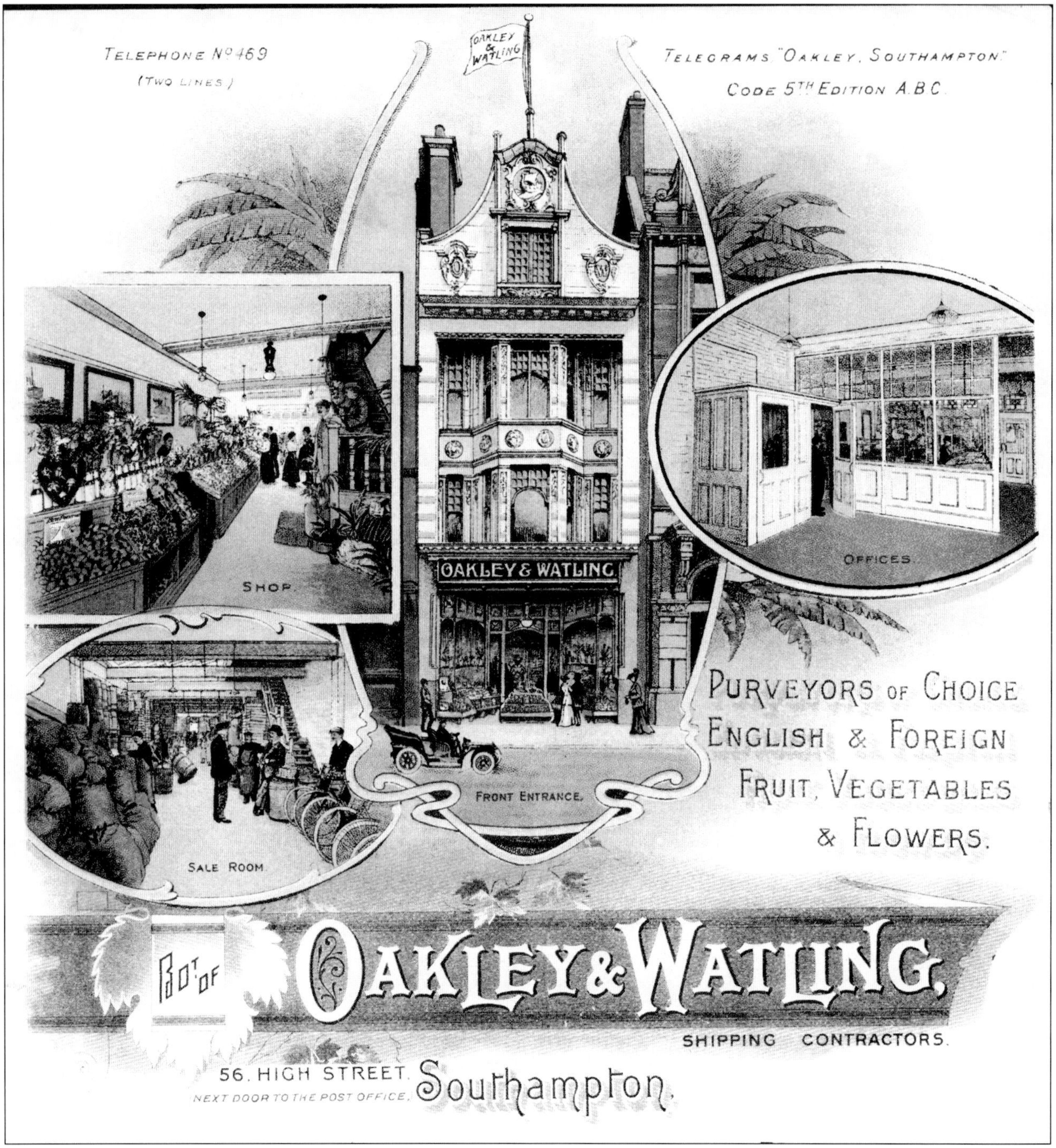

ABOVE: Oakley and Watling, fruit, flower and vegetable wholesalers and retailers, were next door to the Post Office at 56 High Street. This bill of 1921 is for the supply of goods to *SY Mariner*. The account for over £29 was two months overdue.

OPPOSITE TOP: Lowman's Bakers of 82 –84 Portswood Road in 1900. The horse-drawn vans are lined up and waiting to be loaded with the day's fresh bread and cakes for delivery. Founded in 1860, the company had many shops around the town and supplied local people for well over 100 years.

OPPOSITE BELOW: One of the bakehouses at 82-84 Portswood Road. The ovens were coal fired and the 'smalls' bakehouse was where the buns and cakes were created.

S.B. LOWMAN & SONS
S.B. LOWMAN & SONS

MR GEORGE DANCE'S COMPANY.
The entire production from the APOLLO THEATRE, LONDON.

ROYAL
PIER
CONCERTS
DANCING

CHAPTER THREE
SOUTHAMPTON AT PLAY

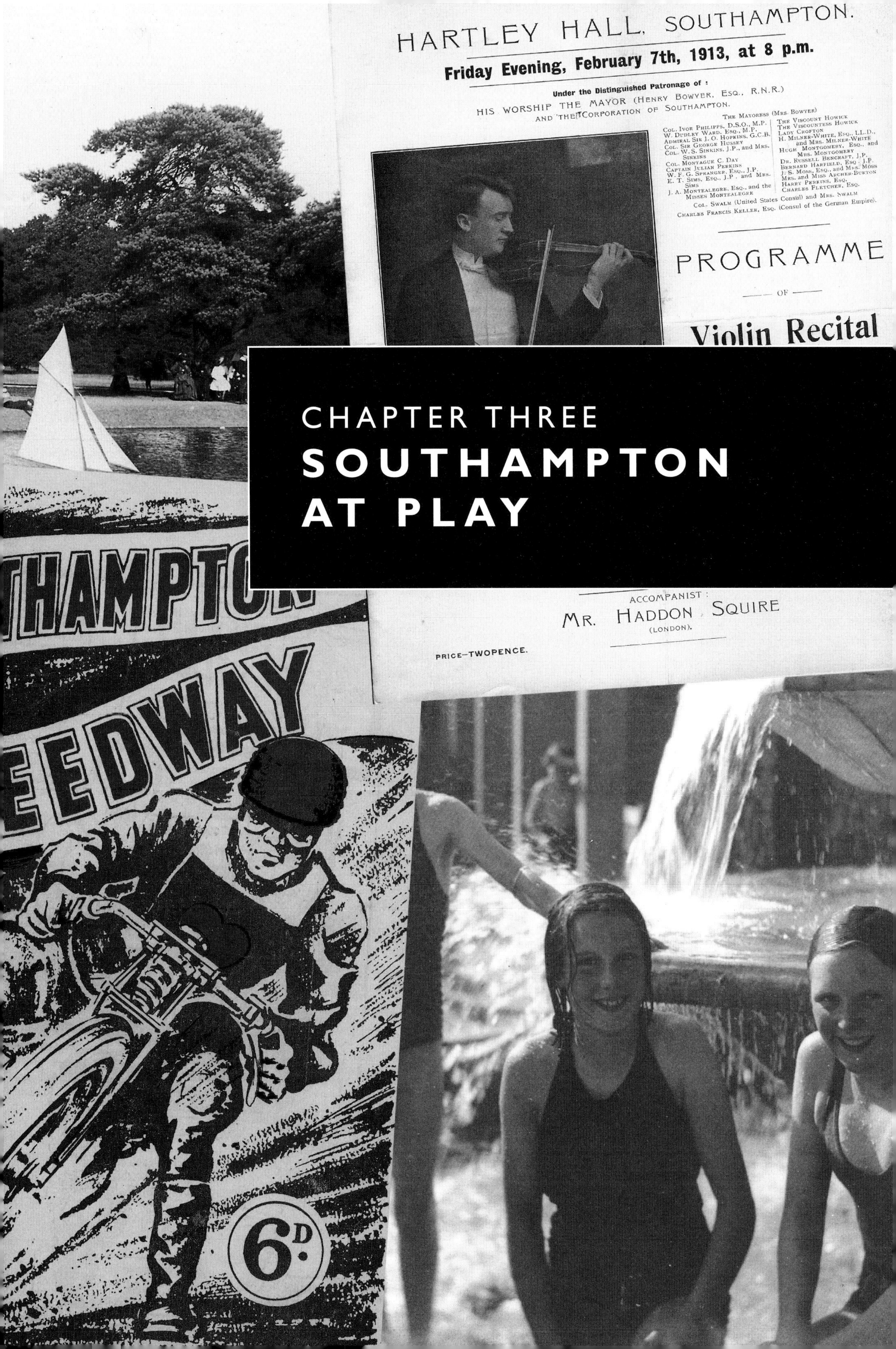

TOP: Weston Shore at the turn of the century. Local people flocked to the beach as soon as the weather was fine enough and this group of mainly women and children are making the most of the sun. In the background is the 'seaweed hut'.

ABOVE: The old 'seaweed hut' on Weston Shore was built in the 1800s mainly of driftwood with a grassed over roof. It was used by boatmen and fishermen as a store and was taken down in the 1960s.

TOP: Western Shore in 1900. A group of onlookers gather as three working horses are taken into the water to cool down. The ladies are in their summer attire topped off with straw hats and parasols to shade their faces from browning in the sun. In the distance are the public baths, the old town walls and the spires of St Michael's and Holy Rood Churches. The land in the foreground was reclaimed in the 1920s and is now the site of the Western Esplanade development.

ABOVE: A crowded summer scene at the Lido on Western Esplanade in the 1930s. Built in the 1890s, the Lido had two covered swimming baths and an outdoor pool that was only open in the summer.

OPPOSITE: Three happy young girls enjoy the fountain at the Lido in the 1930s. These popular baths were eventually closed down in the 1970s and now a shopping centre occupies the site.

TOP: The Royal Pier in 1913. Outside the railway station a military band is playing. Trains would meet the paddle-steamers that ran to the Isle of Wight, Portsmouth and Bournemouth. The Royal Pier was opened in 1833 by Princess Victoria and in 1898 a new pontoon extension was opened. Today only the domed entrance, added in the 1930s, remains.

ABOVE: This 1930s view is from the Royal Pier looking towards the Royal Southern Yacht Club at the corner of Bugle Street. The Royal Pier Hotel was a casualty of war-time bombing, but the warehouse next door and the yacht club building survive today.

ROYAL PIER

SOUTHAMPTON.

Concerts and Entertainments

SEPTEMBER, 1912.

Sunday, Sept. 1st,
at 8 p.m.
Pier Toll 2d., including admission to Pavilion.

The County Borough Police Band

***Monday, Sept. 2nd,**
and during the Week,
at 8 p.m.

MATINEES—
Wednesday & Saturday
at 3.30 p.m. Pier Toll, 1d.
Pavilion, 1/-, 6d., 3d.

First Visit of the Celebrated Costume Concert Party,

THE WAGS

(From the Savoy Theatre, London.)

In their entirely Original Repertoire.

Sunday, Sept. 8th,
at 8 p.m.
Pier Toll 2d., including admission to Pavilion.

The Band of the 5th Hants Regt. (T).

Monday, Sept. 9th,
8 to 10.30 p.m.
PIER TOLL, 1d., PAVILION, 6d.

Dancing in the Pavilion

THE TEMPERANCE BAND.

***Wednesday, Sept. 11th,**
at 3.30 & 7.30 p.m.
Pier Toll ... 1d.
Pavilion ... 6d.
Tickets purchased before day of Concerts include Pier Toll.

Last Appearance this season of the Splendid String Band of H.M.

ROYAL GARRISON ARTILLERY.

(Portsmouth). Conductor - Mr. Chas. Lee.

Vocalist - - Miss ALICE HUMPHRIES (Soprano.)

***Saturday, Sept. 14th,**
at 8 p.m.
Pier Toll ... 1d.
Pavilion, 3s., 2s., & 1s.
One Night Only!
No Pier Toll on Carriages.

MR.

ALBERT CHEVALIER'S RECITALS.

SUPPORTED BY

Miss Tresilian Davy (Soprano.) & Mr. J. C. Holliday. (Solo Pianist and Accompanist.)

Sunday, Sept. 15th,
at 8 p.m.
Pier Toll .. 2d.
Including admission to Pavilion.

The South Hants Temperance Band

The Bands by kind permission of the Commanding Officers.

The Engagement of the Portsmouth and other Military Bands is subject to the exigencies of the Service.

This Programme is subject to Alteration. Other Performances will be duly announced. Smoking Permitted in Pavilion.

OPPOSITE: A poster advertising the Royal Pier programme of concerts and entertainments in September 1912. Military bands in particular played regularly. The Pier was a very popular venue for concerts and weekly dances were held in the Pavilion.

TOP: The guardians of the Royal Pier around 1910. The gentlemen are two ticket collectors, a policeman and the pier superintendent posing for the photographer at the pier's entrance. The 'Sun-Rays' were performing at the Pier Theatre.

ABOVE: The Royal Pier circa 1949 with Cunard's *Aquitania* steaming past. On the left is the *Vecta* or *Balmoral* ferry to the Isle of Wight To the right are some of the last paddle-steamers. The reclaimed land on the right has not yet been developed into Mayflower Park. Note the stop-me-and-buy-one ice-cream seller.

LEFT: Built in 1898, the New Grand Theatre at the Marlands headlined some of the most famous music hall artistes. Later plays and pantomimes were produced and in the declining years of the 1950s, strip shows were the mainstay. The building was demolished in 1959 and the site is now occupied by shops and the Southampton Tourist Information Centre.

OPPOSITE: Grand Theatre pantomime advertisement for Mother Goose in December 1957.

BELOW: A Grand Theatre programme for May 1938. *The Merry Wives of Windsor* was being performed by the Civic Players, Southampton's own repertory company, which was considered one of the finest in the country. Admission prices varied from 9d (4p) for the pit, 1s 6d (7.5p) for stalls and 2s (10p) for the circle. A box for four could be had for 10s 6d (52.5p) As a result of the popularity of 'talkies' at the cinema, live theatre had been suffering from declining numbers during the previous ten years. However, in 1938, the Grand was still packing in 4,000 keen theatre-goers every week.

ABOVE: Advertising card for the London cast of Mr George Dance's Company performing Veronique, circa 1900.

GRAND THEATRE CIVIC CENTRE SOUTHAMPTON

MANAGER & LICENSEE
RAYMOND 'TUBBY' BENNET

TELEPHONE
26651

DIRECTION
F. J. BUTTERWORTH

FULLY LICENSED BARS IN ALL PARTS

For a Resident Season of Four Weeks from December 23rd

Week Commencing Monday December 23rd
" " " " 30th
" " " January 6th

DAILY AT 2.30 & 6 p.m.

Week Commencing Monday January 13th **NIGHTLY** at 6 p.m.
With Matinees on WED., THURS. and SAT. at 2.30 p.m.

A Feast of Fun for Old and Young

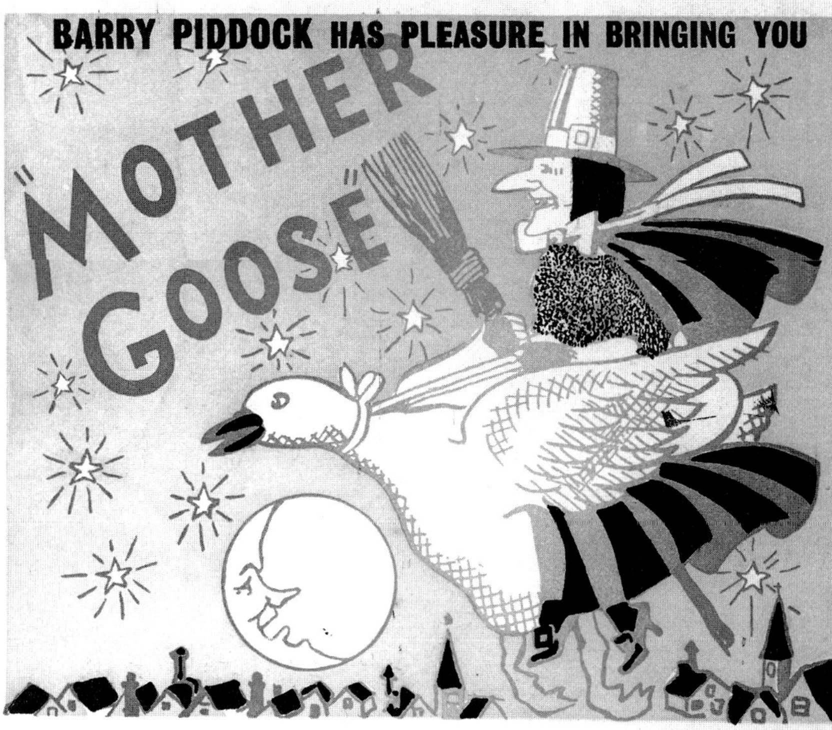

A Real Xmas Treat for the Whole Family

WITH ALL THE TRADITIONAL CHARACTERS
INCLUDING

"PRISCILLA" - THE GOOSE "MOTHER GOOSE" - HERSELF "HER DAUGHTER" - JILL HER SON - "TUBBY" THE "BROKERS MEN" THE "SQUIRE" "DEMON AND FAIRY" THE HERO "COLIN" THE GOOD FAIRY

SPECIALITIES BY NICO FERRY AND PARTNER THE HUMAN FROG
HOLLOWAY AND PAT COLLINS AND JACKSON ANETTE AND NOELE
FULL CORPS DE BALLET OF CHILDREN & VILLAGERS

PRICES OF ADMISSION

Stalls 5/- 4/- 3/- Circle 4/- Upper Circle 2/-

ALL SEATS BOOKABLE IN ADVANCE

PATRONS BOOKING MORE THAN TEN SEATS FOR ANY PERFORMANCE WILL BE GIVEN ONE FREE SEAT IN EVERY TEN SO BOOKED AND PAID FOR IN ADVANCE

GRAND THEATRE CIVIC CENTRE Southampton
WINDMILL OF THE SOUTH
Direction–F. J. Butterworth
Manager & Licensee–Frederick Rhyman
Phone 26651
MONDAY, MARCH 30th, 1959
6-25 – TWICE NIGHTLY – 8-35
CYRIL DOWLER presents
BRITAIN'S LATEST AND GREATEST STRIP STAR
The Fabulous
RHODA ROGERS
FEATURED IN
STRIP-TEASE CHA-CHA
The Very Latest in Saucy Daring Presentations
Wriggle Dancers
Local Nudes
and Fan Dancers
CYRIL DOWLER YOUR HOST
Christine & Colin CAMPBELL
Music Maestros Please !
See– Southampton's Saucy Strippers
TONIA GALE
A VOICE IN A MILLION
RON DILLON
AND ALL STAR CAST
CONFESSIONS OF A FAN DANCER !
THE GLAMOUROUS AND BEAUTIFUL
INTERNATIONAL NUDES
CAN YOU POSE
THE ART AND CHARM– OF A "STRIPPER"
George Allen (Printers) Ltd., Brimington, Chesterfield

RIGHT: This weekly edition of *What's On* for March 1932 advertises that on the screen of the Empire Theatre was Constance Bennet in *Common Law* and on the stage were the Welsh Miners Quartette. Built in 1928 the Empire in Commercial Road became the Gaumont in 1950 and later still, in 1987, the Mayflower Theatre which is still popular and attracting audiences from far and wide.

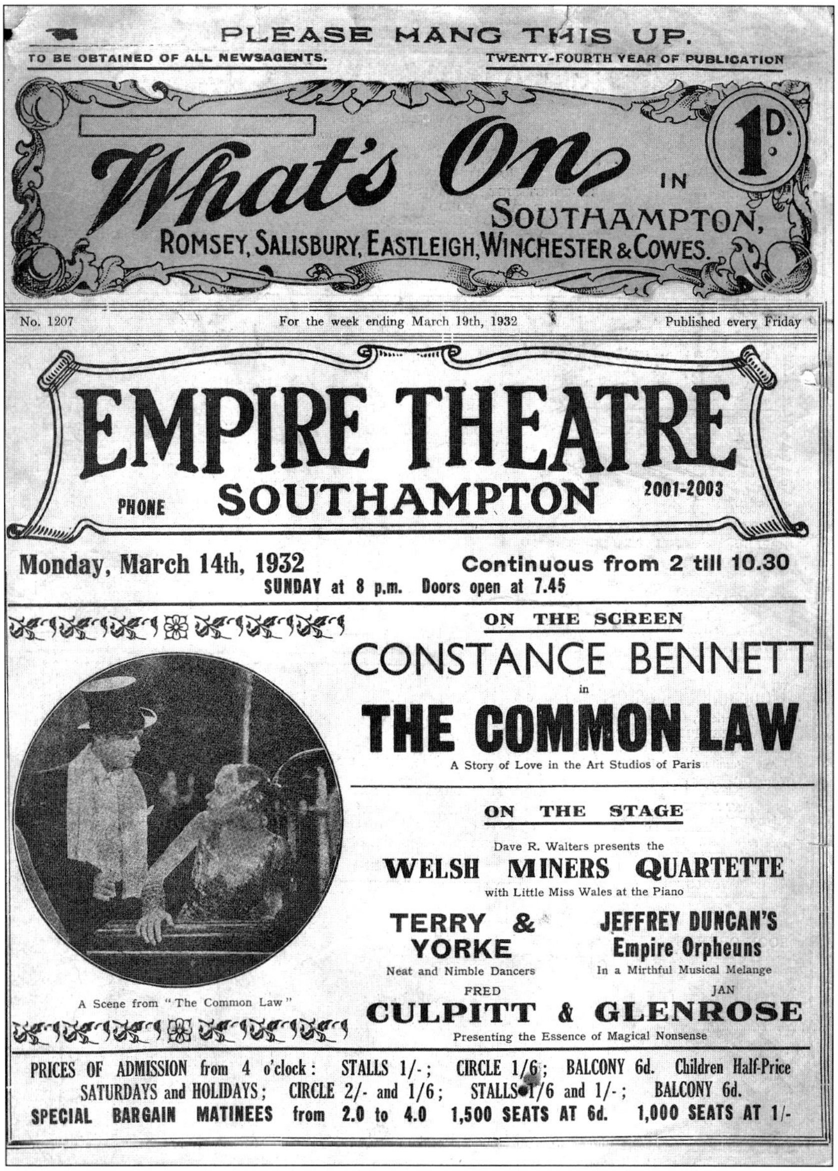

OPPOSITE: An advertisement for the Grand Theatre towards the end of its life. The theatre had a long illustrious career of over sixty years as one of the town's prime entertainment establishments. Unfortunately, one of the last shows before closure and demolition was of the less illustrious kind – *Strip-tease Cha-Cha*, featuring Rhoda Rogers.

RIGHT: A Vaudeville programme in aid of the Southampton Division of the British Red Cross held in the New Pear Tree Hall in June 1940. The list of entertainers included the Cossack Sisters on Piano Accordions and Betty Dunbar, the 'Queen of Comedy'. The Southampton Division were keen to encourage men aged between 40 and 50 to volunteer to train as stretcher bearers for wartime duty. Training classes were held on Friday evenings at the Hants and Dorset Bus Company garage in Grosvenor Square.

EMPIRE
THEATRE
BUGLE STREET, NEAR ROYAL PIER, SOUTHAMPTON.
TRAMS TO ROYAL PIER.
6-30 | TWICE NIGHTLY | 8-40
WEEK COMMENCING MAY 4
Special Starring Engagement of that Great London Dramatic Co.
MOSS'S SELECTED PLAYERS.
MONDAY, TUESDAY & WEDNESDAY.
The Great Moral Drama
ONLY SOILED
Full of Excellent Comedy and Pathos.
THUR. FRI. & SAT.
The Ever Popular Irish Drama
THE
COLLEEN BAWN
Special Scenery and Effects, Songs and Dances.
PICTURE PROGRAMME SUNDAY NEXT 8-0 till 10-0 p.m.
Licensed Bars to all parts of the Theatre.
PEOPLE'S POPULAR PRICES
BOXES 2/6 to seat four 10/-
STALLS 1/0
CIRCLE 1/0
PIT-STALLS 6d.
PIT 3d.
Box Office open 10 a.m. to 10 p.m. No extra charge for booking. Phone 5338 Children Half Price.

OPPOSITE: Poster for the Empire Theatre in Bugle Street in 1920. Built in 1886, the theatre was converted into a cinema in 1908 and was closed and demolished in 1925.

SOUTHAMPTON'S PREMIER ENTERTAINMENT HOUSE

HIPPODROME

SOUTHAMPTON

PROPRIETORS - THE SOUTH OF ENGLAND HIPPODROMES, LTD.
CHAIRMAN & MANAGING DIRECTOR - MR. CHARLES GULLIVER
RESIDENT MANAGER - - - - - - - GEO. H. STAMMERS

THURSDAY (2nd House), APRIL 26th, 1923

MAURETANIA NIGHT

S.S. "MAURETANIA"

GALA PERFORMANCE

UNDER THE PATRONAGE OF THE DIRECTORS OF THE CUNARD LINE, AND THE COMMANDER, OFFICERS AND MEN OF THE S.S. "MAURETANIA"

RIGHT: The Hippodrome Theatre, Ogle Road. A 'Mauretania Night' programme. Performed for the officers and crew of *RMS Mauretania*, this 1923 special event presented a selection of music, song and skits. All aboard by 8.20, sailing at 8.30 and berthing by 11.45pm. An additional attraction was the bright and breezy 'Mauretania Boys', who added their talents to the evening with songs and comedy. The theatre also ran *Berengaria* and *Aquitania* evenings.

RIGHT: The interior of the Hippodrome Theatre in Ogle Road. The sign on the right announces that church services were held at the Hippodrome at 8.15pm. Opened in 1883 as the Prince of Wales Theatre, it specialised in variety shows until the theatre closed in 1939.

HARTLEY HALL, SOUTHAMPTON.

Friday Evening, February 7th, 1913, at 8 p.m.

Under the Distinguished Patronage of :

HIS WORSHIP THE MAYOR (HENRY BOWYER, ESQ., R.N.R.)
AND THE CORPORATION OF SOUTHAMPTON.

THE MAYORESS (MRS. BOWYER)

COL. IVOR PHILIPPS, D.S.O., M.P.	THE VISCOUNT HOWICK
W. DUDLEY WARD, ESQ., M.P.	THE VISCOUNTESS HOWICK
ADMIRAL SIR J. O. HOPKINS, G.C.B.	LADY CROFTON
COL. SIR GEORGE HUSSEY	H. MILNER-WHITE, ESQ., LL.D., and MRS. MILNER-WHITE
COL. W. S. SINKINS, J.P., and MRS. SINKINS	HUGH MONTGOMERY, ESQ., and MRS. MONTGOMERY
COL. MONTAGUE C. DAY	DR. RUSSELL BENCRAFT, J.P.
CAPTAIN JULIAN PERKINS	BERNARD HARFIELD, ESQ., J.P.
W. F. G. SPRANGER, ESQ., J.P.	J. S. MOSS, ESQ., and MRS. MOSS
E. T. SIMS, ESQ., J.P., and MRS. SIMS	MRS. and MISS ARCHER-BURTON
J. A. MONTEALEGRE, ESQ., and the MISSES MONTEALEGRE	HARRY PERKINS, ESQ.
	CHARLES FLETCHER, ESQ.

COL. SWALM (United States Consul) and MRS. SWALM
CHARLES FRANCIS KELLER, ESQ. (Consul of the German Empire).

PROGRAMME
OF
Violin Recital
BY
EDGAR MOUNCHER

Photo by A. Meyer Schein, Vienna.

ASSISTED BY
MISS ELISE LOUBERT.
MEZZO SOPRANO
(Of Hammerstein's London Opera House, Season 1912).

ACCOMPANIST :
MR. HADDON SQUIRE
(LONDON).

LEFT: The programme for a violin recital by Edgar Mouncher at the Hartley Hall in High Street in 1913. The hall was part of the Hartley Institute and was used for concerts and lectures. The Hartley Institute later moved to Highfield and evolved into the University of Southampton. Although Highfield is still the main campus, there are several faculties located around the city.

BELOW: The opening programme for the Broadway Cinema in Portswood Road on June 6, 1930. The opening film was Rookery Nook, an Aldwych farce starring Ralph Lynn and Tom Walls. Successful as a cinema until the 1960s, the Broadway became a bingo hall in 1963. In 2002 it is still pulling in the bingo crowds.

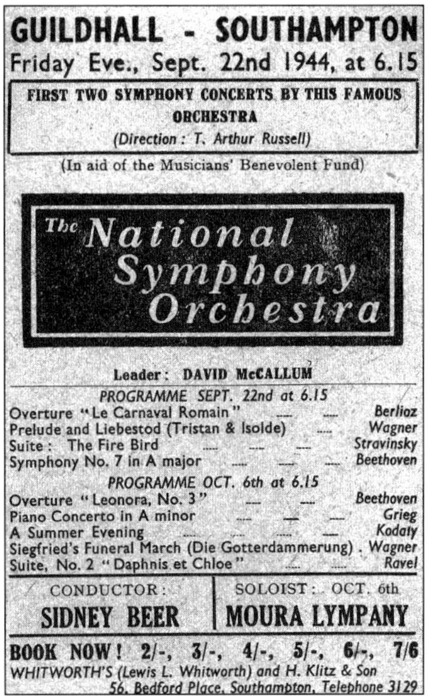

GUILDHALL - SOUTHAMPTON
Friday Eve., Sept. 22nd 1944, at 6.15

FIRST TWO SYMPHONY CONCERTS BY THIS FAMOUS ORCHESTRA
(Direction : T. Arthur Russell)

(In aid of the Musicians' Benevolent Fund)

The National Symphony Orchestra

Leader : DAVID McCALLUM

PROGRAMME SEPT. 22nd at 6.15

Overture "Le Carnaval Romain"	*Berlioz*
Prelude and Liebestod (Tristan & Isolde)	*Wagner*
Suite : The Fire Bird	*Stravinsky*
Symphony No. 7 in A major	*Beethoven*

PROGRAMME OCT. 6th at 6.15

Overture "Leonora, No. 3"	*Beethoven*
Piano Concerto in A minor	*Grieg*
A Summer Evening	*Kodaly*
Siegfried's Funeral March (Die Gotterdammerung)	*Wagner*
Suite, No. 2 "Daphnis et Chloe"	*Ravel*

CONDUCTOR :	SOLOIST : OCT. 6th
SIDNEY BEER	MOURA LYMPANY

BOOK NOW! 2/-, 3/-, 4/-, 5/-, 6/-, 7/6
WHITWORTH'S (Lewis L. Whitworth) and H. Klitz & Son
56, Bedford Place, Southampton, Telephone 3129

ABOVE: A Guildhall programme for a concert by the National Symphony Orchestra in 1944, in aid of the Musicians' Benevolent Fund.

RIGHT: The Regal Cinema in 1941. This was one of the occasions that a matinee performance of a variety show was held in aid of the Mayor's Air Raid Distress Fund. Top of the bill was George Formby.

REGAL CINEMA, Southampton

TUESDAY, JUNE 10 at 2.30

Doors Open at 1.45

FLYING VISIT OF

GEORGE FORMBY WITH BERYL

and All-Star Variety Programme

in aid of

THE MAYOR OF SOUTHAMPTON'S

AIR RAID DISTRESS FUND

STALLS 2/6 O 12

BELOW: The Regal Cinema in Above Bar. The cinema was opened in 1934 by Gracie Fields and Captain Arthur Rostron. In 1912 as Captain of *SS Carpathia*, he brought his ship to the rescue of the *Titanic's* survivors. The cinema had seats for 1,700 people and in 1945 was acquired as one of the Odeon cinemas. The building was demolished in 1995 to make way for shops. Madame Spy with Fay Wray was showing with John Howlett at the Wonder Organ. To the right is the Church of Christ and on the left the Portland Arms.

TOP: The East Street Wesleyan Brotherhood brass band proudly posing for the photographer in 1904. The Wesleyan Chapel was next to Edwin Jones's shops at 29-34 East Street.

ABOVE: A photograph of Southampton Citadel Young Persons' Band taken before a visit to Portsmouth North in 1932. The notice on the wall is optimistically calling for 200 new students for Bible classes.

TOP: A group of scouts outside the South Western Hotel in the 1920s. Special scout cruises sailed from Southampton in the 1920s and 1930s to Scout Jamborees in Norway and the Baltic countries.

ABOVE: Yachts on the boating lake on the Common, 1912. This was a very popular hobby, especially at weekends, when yacht races took place. Many a yacht was becalmed and the hapless owner might wait, sometimes for hours, for the yacht to come within reach. Today these type of yachts are collectors' pieces.

TOP: A summer's day at the paddling pool on the Common, some time in the late 1940s. As the photo shows, this pool was – and still is – extremely popular in hot weather.

ABOVE: At the fair on the Common in 1912, the steam galloper roundabout has some happy young girls on board. The first fair was held on the Common in 1860 and today the tradition continues on bank holidays.

ABOVE: One of the many rowing clubs in the town. There was a club at West Quay and at Crosshouse. Boats could also be hired from Dyers at Cobden Bridge.

RIGHT: West Quay Regatta Race Fixtures for 1916. The race commenced outside the clubhouse with a route to Cracknore Hard, around two buoys and back. The entrance fee was 1s (5p).

West Regatta Quay Club.

PRÆ CETERIS

CLUB HOUSE, WEST QUAY, SOUTHAMPTON.

Commodore ...	TANKERVILLE CHAMBERLAYNE, ESQ.
Vice-Commodore	JOHN HARFIELD BOYES, Esq.
Rear-Commodore	LIEUT.-COL. SIR G. A. E. HUSSEY.
Hon. Treasurer ...	CHARLES J. BEATON, Esq.
Secretary ...	WILLIS BAILEY.

RACE FIXTURES, 1916.

Chairman of Sailing Committee—**Mr. F. HOLE.**

Handicapper—**Mr. C. J. PARSONS.**

The Committee reserve the right to cancel any dates, or of making any alteration in this Programme which they may deem expedient.

A Series of OPEN HANDICAP RACES for YACHTS, 3 Tons and under, will be held off the Club House, West Quay, on SATURDAY AFTERNOONS.

TOP: The Bowling Green in Orchard Place near God's House Tower. Still in use today, it was founded in 1299 and is the oldest bowling green in the world. This 1931 photograph shows the club house with a Cunarder in the Floating Dry Dock in the background.

ABOVE: Bowlers at the Southampton Bowling Green. This is one of a set of photographs recording a tournament in 1931.

OPPOSITE: The Commissionaire from the Southampton Skating Rink that stood in Shirley Road from 1915-22. This was a very popular roller skating rink with local people. During the First World War the building was used to house German prisoners-of-war.

SOUTHAMPTON RINK
EXIT
EXIT
PHOTO

OFFICIAL PROGRAMME
TWOPENCE
THE SPORTSDROME
SOUTHAMPTON
(General Manager—Capt. A. PRINCE-COX)
Boxing Tournament
MONDAY, DECEMBER 11th
1939
Doors open 6-30 p.m. — Commence 7-30 p.m.
SPORTSDROME
RINK
ROLLER SKATING
each evening
6 p.m. to 10 p.m.
Afternoon Session
Saturdays 2-30 to 5 p.m.
One Shilling
SPORTSDROME
BALLROOM
DANCING
each evening
7 p.m. to 10 p.m.
GIL HULME'S BAND
One Shilling

Grand Twenty-First
Anniversary Meeting
SOUTHAMPTON
SPEEDWAY
Tuesday, October 11th, 1949
OFFICIAL PROGRAMME :: PRICE ONE SHILLING

OPPOSITE ABOVE: The Southampton Civil Service Touring Team pose for their photograph after their match at Ventnor on the Isle of Wight in the summer of 1929.

OPPOSITE BELOW LEFT: A boxing tournament at the Sportsdome at Bannister Court in Court Road, December 11, 1939. The main event was between Arthur Danahar, of Bethnal Green, an ex-lightweight champion, and George Odwell, the contender for the title. Lightweights Pte Spike Robson, of Southampton, and Johnny Ware, of Bournemouth, faced each other in the ring. All-in team wrestling was also held at the Sportsdome.

OPPOSITE BELOW RIGHT: Southampton 'Saints' speedway programme for the 21st anniversary meeting. Speedway was held at the Bannister Court Stadium from its launch in 1928 until the 1960s. The final meeting of the season was a major event with a firework display as the grand finale. The Stadium was demolished in the 1960s to make way for housing.

ABOVE: The Saints' 1949 speedway team (left to right, back row) Frank Goulden (manager), Bill Thatcher, Phil Bishop, Peter Bantock, Cecil Bailey, Alf Kaines, Bill Rogers, Jimmy Baxter, Bill Griffiths, Roy Craighead and (front) Jim Squibb, Bob Oakley (captain) and Tom Oakley.

ABOVE: The programme for the May 30, 1950, meeting, the second leg of the *Daily Mail* National Trophy Competition, with Southampton versus Edinburgh. The following week the Saints took on Plymouth. At that time the track record for four laps of the 333-yard Southampton track (clutch start) was 64.4 seconds, set by Bob Oakley of Southampton on May 23, 1950.

RIGHT: The cover of the menu for the Press Ball was drawn by The Echo's long-standing cartoonist, Oz, who regularly brought a smile to readers' faces over the years. The 1955 ball was held at the Polygon Hotel. Some of the delicacies on offer were consomme paysanne, loin of lamb primeurs and fruit salad Polygon. Dinner commenced at 7.30 with a cabaret at 11.30pm. The comedian Harold Berens delighted the audience, as did a troupe of dancers from the Windmill Theatre, London.

Press Ball
PRESS
PRESS
SOUTHAMPTON 1955
EXPENSES
To Hire of Rickshaw
Entert

"White Star" "Welcome"
Decorations.
Southampton C.E.&Co.REG.
H.P. Jupp

KING EDW

HE CHURCH CONGRESS, 1913
PASSING THROUGH THE BARGATE.
DAILY MAIL PHOTOGRAPH.

CHAPTER FOUR
SPECIAL DAYS

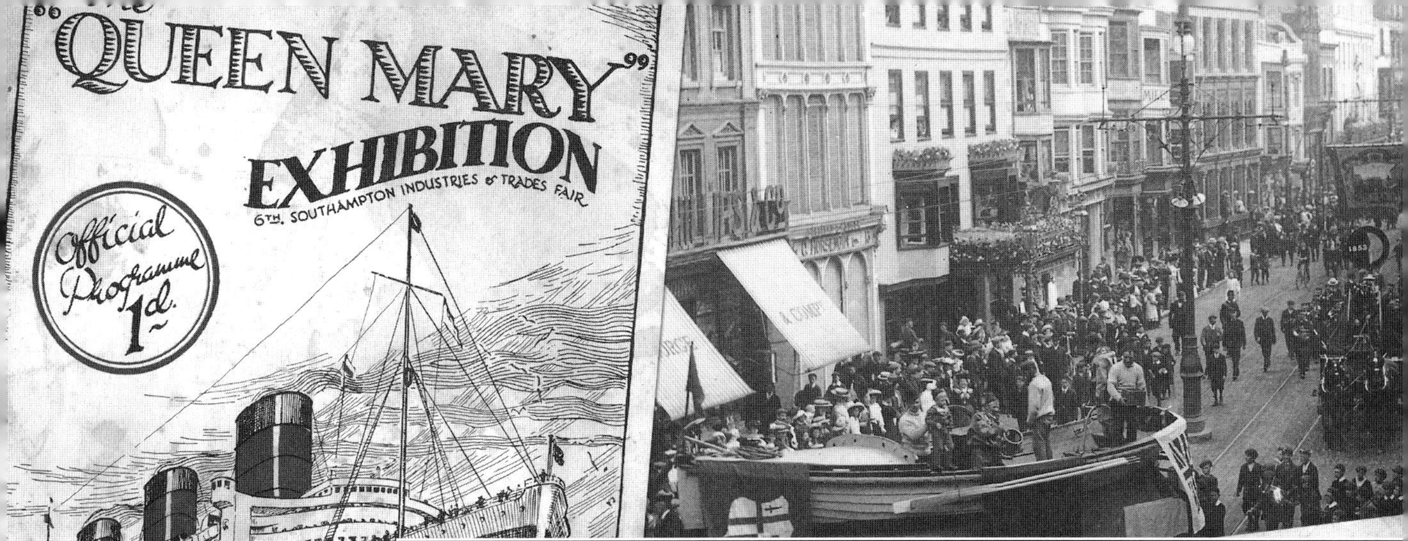

ABOVE: In 1907 White Star Line moved their main operations from Liverpool to Southampton. The town was delighted as this meant more business for local companies and more work for the people. A new dock was to be built to accommodate large new ships like the *Olympic* and *Titanic*. The building festooned with flags is the Hudson Brothers' Provision Store at Market Chambers, High Street.

TOP: Hundreds of people, dressed in their Sunday best, attended a King Edward memorial service at the Marlands on May 20, 1910. The Grand Theatre is in the background.

ABOVE: The Albion Congregational Church in St Mary's Street, built in 1848, could accommodate up to 1,100. This photograph shows the church congregation at the Indian Empire Bazaar of 1909, held at the Coliseum Skating Rink, previously the Victoria Hall, in Portland Terrace.

TOP: Every year a lifeboat demonstration was held to raise money for the lifeboatmen. This photograph shows the parade winding down the High Street past the Crown Hotel with George Phillips & Co the stationers on the left

ABOVE: During ten days in June 1914 the St Mary's Tudor Pageant took place in the grounds of The Deanery. The new church spire had been completed and at the end of the pageant, the new bells were consecrated and rung for the first time.

ABOVE: The Church Congress procession passing through the Bargate in 1913, en route to a large exhibition being held on the Marlands. Southampton welcomed thousands of visitors and delegates for a week-long series of events. Special services were held at St Mary's, St. Luke's and All Saints Churches.

TOP: May Day singing on top of the Bargate, 1912. The choir of St Mary's and what looks like half the townsfolk, rise early to take part in a tradition that goes back to the 17th century. Today the tradition is continued by the choir of King Edward's School.

ABOVE: The children of Northam Council Schools welcome a large party of French dignitaries on a civic visit to the town in May 1913.

RIGHT AND BELOW: At the end of the First World War memorials were erected around Britain. On November 6, 1920, the Cenotaph War Memorial, designed by Sir Edwin Lutyens, was unveiled in Southampton. The base of the memorial is covered in wreaths and flowers.

TOP: HRH The Prince of Wales on his way to perform the opening ceremony of the new Floating Dry Dock on June 27, 1924. Travelling down the High Street past the Dolphin Hotel and just by Holyrood Church, he passes under a banner that declares 'Long Live Our Prince'.

ABOVE: His Royal Highness with his entourage just entering the Dry Dock. After opening the dock, a civic reception was held to commemorate the occasion. The dock fell into disuse in 1933 and was subsequently sold.

TOP: Ivy Road, St Denys. A group of happy young women make their way to St Denys Church for the Church Fete in 1921.

ABOVE: In March 1929 Lord Jellicoe visited Southampton to receive the freedom of the town. After the official presentation, he attended a civic luncheon in his honour held on board the White Star Liner *SS Olympic*.

TOP: The 'Hospital Carnival' week in 1933 was organised to raise funds for the town's hospital. This photograph shows 4,000 schoolchildren doing synchronised gymnastics at the Stadium in Bannister Park.

ABOVE: A float for the jubilee pageant declares: 'Southampon the port that links the world'. The names of shipping companies proudly displayed include Royal Mail, Cunard Whitestar, Canadian Pacific and Union Castle Lines.

OPPOSITE RIGHT: Coronation Souvenir 1937. The country has a new king and queen – King George VI and Queen Elizabeth – and this commemorative booklet of their story was presented to customers as a complimentary souvenir by Edwin Jones & Co.

LEFT: The official Silver Jubilee programme, 1935. A large procession took place from the Civic Centre to the Common where a pageant was held. The Jubilee was also celebrated by the presentation of a medal to local schoolchildren and the allocation of £300 for boots and shoes for children of the poor.

RIGHT: The Southampton Industries and Trades Fair entitled 'The Queen Mary Exhibition'. The sixth fair of this kind was held from October 5-12, 1935, at the Coliseum in Portland Terrace. Various local companies gave demonstrations of their trades which included cigarette-making, cigar-rolling, butter-making, health cookery and hairdressing. There were also many local companies with trade stands including Imperial Airways, Thorneycrofts and Southern Newspapers.

ABOVE: A catalogue for the Queen Mary Exhibition in 1938. This exhibition was part of the King George V Silver Jubilee celebrations and on display was a 22ft model of the new *RMS Queen Mary*. The same model can now be seen in Southampton's Maritime Museum.

MERCHANT
NAVY WEEK
SOUTHAMPTON
JULY 17 TO 24
GY 741
GY 741
KENNETH SHOESMITH
OFFICIAL
SOUVENIR HANDBOOK
AND
PROGRAMME OF EVENTS.
SIXPENCE

LEFT: Festival of Britain 1951. Britain was still recovering from the ravages of war. Designed to put the whole country on show to the people of Britain and the world, the festival celebrated the 'best of British'. Southampton held four exhibitions with the main one devoted, as might be expected, to shipping and industry. The exhibition was held from June 30 to July 14 at the Blighmont Hall in Millbrook.

RIGHT: A Coronation Carnival programme for 1953. The Carnival attracted thousands who lined the route from the Common, down The Avenue, to The Bargate and along High Street to the Royal Pier. The Coronation Carnival was an evening event which started at 7.30pm. At the finish of the procession a fun fair was in operation and the evening drew to a close with a firework display off the Royal Pier.

OPPOSITE: Merchant Navy Week, July 1937. A series of exhibits and practical displays was held in Sheds 107 and 108 in the docks. Warships and ocean liners were also open for inspection by the public, including *HMS Resolution* and *HMS Southampton*, *RMS Aquitania*, *Asturias*, *Empress of Britain*, *Queen Mary* and *Warwick Castle*.

ABOVE: A group of children gathered to have their photograph taken during coronation celebrations in 1953. Perhaps the photographer has broken up the party, as few are smiling and many look like reluctant subjects. Several of the boys have been lucky enough to get their souvenir Brooke Bond tea union flag hats.

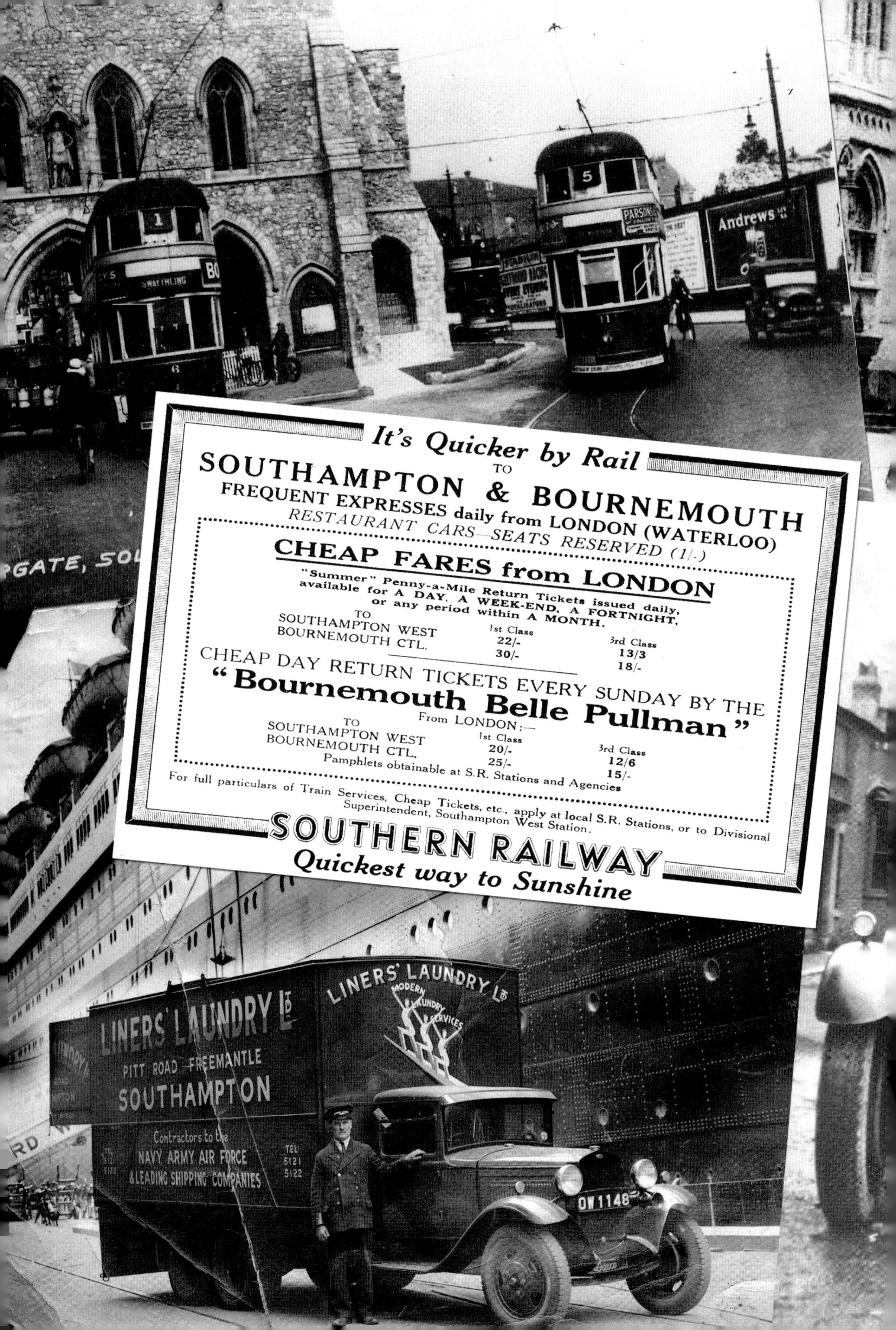
SWAYTHLING
PARSONS
Andrews
STADIUM
It's Quicker by Rail
TO
SOUTHAMPTON & BOURNEMOUTH
FREQUENT EXPRESSES daily from LONDON (WATERLOO)
RESTAURANT CARS—SEATS RESERVED (1/-)
CHEAP FARES from LONDON
"Summer" Penny-a-Mile Return Tickets issued daily, available for A DAY, A WEEK-END, A FORTNIGHT, or any period within A MONTH.
TO
SOUTHAMPTON WEST 1st Class 22/- 3rd Class 13/3
BOURNEMOUTH CTL. 30/- 18/-
CHEAP DAY RETURN TICKETS EVERY SUNDAY BY THE
"Bournemouth Belle Pullman"
From LONDON:—
TO
SOUTHAMPTON WEST 1st Class 20/- 3rd Class 12/6
BOURNEMOUTH CTL. 25/- 15/-
Pamphlets obtainable at S.R. Stations and Agencies
For full particulars of Train Services, Cheap Tickets, etc., apply at local S.R. Stations, or to Divisional Superintendent, Southampton West Station.
SOUTHERN RAILWAY
Quickest way to Sunshine
LINERS' LAUNDRY LTD
MODERN LAUNDRY SERVICES
LINERS' LAUNDRY LTD
PITT ROAD FREEMANTLE
SOUTHAMPTON
Contractors to the
NAVY ARMY AIR FORCE
& LEADING SHIPPING COMPANIES
TEL: 5121 5122
OW 1148

CHAPTER FIVE

SOUTHAMPTON ON THE MOVE

TOP: The junction of New Road and Above Bar Street, an open top tram is travelling past the clock tower heading towards the High Street and the Docks. Horse drawn trams were introduced to the town in 1879 with the first electric trams making an appearance in 1900. They were a very reliable and well used form of public transport for half-a-century and ran until 1949.

ABOVE: Two dome-topped trams pass at the Bargate in the 1930s. The number one to Swaythling is just about to go through the Bargate arch and the number five to the Floating Bridge passes by, on the way down the High Street. The dome-topped tram was unique to Southampton and was designed in order that two decked trams could pass under the arch of the Bargate. The increasing amount of traffic in the town centre resulted in the demolition of buildings first on one side of the Bargate and later on the other side to create a new road. The result is that the Bargate is now situated on its own 'island' with a paved surround – ideal for pedestrians to enjoy this ancient building.

RIGHT: From 1949 onwards buses have been the main form of public transport around Southampton. This photograph shows a 1952 red Guy Arab Southampton Corporation bus, one of a fleet that operated on all routes around the town. As it heads through Bassett, the number 15A proudly displays the city centre as its destination not long after the town was awarded city status.

BELOW: One of Southampton Corporation's steam lorries around 1906. Capable of carrying up to eight tons, the lorry also had the capacity to tip its load. A few years later steam lorries would be superseded by the more reliable and cheaper petrol lorry.

GENERAL HAULAGE CONTRACTOR WALTER WEBB
WALTER WEBB SOUTHAMPTON
WALTER WEBB SOUTHAMPTON.
M-4513

LINERS' LAUNDRY LTD
PITT ROAD FREEMANTLE
SOUTHAMPTON
Contractors to the
NAVY. ARMY. AIR FORCE
&LEADING SHIPPING COMPANIES
TEL 5121 5122
LINERS' LAUNDRY LTD
MODERN LAUNDRY SERVICES
OW 1148

OPPOSITE: A Liners' Laundry van photographed by the side of the Queen Mary in the 1930s. Liners' Laundry were based in Pitt Road, Freemantle and were the main contractor to the major shipping companies. Publicity photographs taken with ocean liners were used by many companies for advertising purposes.

OPPOSITE TOP: Mr Walter Webb's fleet of Foden steam waggons, lined up in 1916 for their photograph to advertise Goodrich solid tyres. Webbs were in business in Bevois Street as general haulage contractors and coal merchants.

ABOVE: A happy child poses for the photographer in front of Dad's lorry, some time in the 1930s. Tagart, Morgan and Coles were timber merchants at Crosshouse Hard.

TOP: This photograph of the West Station, built in 1895, was taken during the first decade of the new century. During very high tides the sea flooded some of the tracks before land reclamation enabled the shoreline to be realigned further from the station. After rebuilding in 1935, the station was renamed Southampton Central.

ABOVE: A Merchant Navy class locomotive waiting at the platform at Ocean Terminal in the Docks. Boat trains from London Waterloo to Southampton Docks were frequent and the Holland America Line headboard on this one distinguishes it as a special service. Judging by the expression on the faces of this family, steam was as fascinating then as it is today.

OPPOSITE TOP: It's Quicker by Rail advertisement.

It's Quicker by Rail
TO

SOUTHAMPTON & BOURNEMOUTH

FREQUENT EXPRESSES daily from LONDON (WATERLOO)

RESTAURANT CARS—SEATS RESERVED (1/-)

CHEAP FARES from LONDON

"Summer" Penny-a-Mile Return Tickets issued daily, available for A DAY, A WEEK-END, A FORTNIGHT, or any period within A MONTH.

TO	1st Class	3rd Class
SOUTHAMPTON WEST	22/-	13/3
BOURNEMOUTH CTL.	30/-	18/-

CHEAP DAY RETURN TICKETS EVERY SUNDAY BY THE

"Bournemouth Belle Pullman"

From LONDON:—

TO	1st Class	3rd Class
SOUTHAMPTON WEST	20/-	12/6
BOURNEMOUTH CTL.	25/-	15/-

Pamphlets obtainable at S.R. Stations and Agencies

For full particulars of Train Services, Cheap Tickets, etc., apply at local S.R. Stations, or to Divisional Superintendent, Southampton West Station.

SOUTHERN RAILWAY

Quickest way to Sunshine

The Hampshire Aeroplane Club

FOUNDED 1926

PRESIDENT: THE RT. HON. LORD LOUIS MOUNTBATTEN, K.C.V.O., R.N.

FLYING TUITION BY QUALIFIED INSTRUCTORS

Flying Rates: Dual Instruction, from **37/6** per hour; Solo Flying, from **27/6** per hour; Air Taxis, **6**d. per mile.

Full particulars from the **MANAGER,** Hampshire Aeroplane Club,
THE AERODROME, SOUTHAMPTON Telephone: **EASTLEIGH 170**

ABOVE: Supermarine Sports and Social Club dance programme for January 6, 1928. The Napier S5 had won the Schneider Trophy for Britain in 1927 and would retain the trophy for good in 1931. Supermarine went on to build the world famous Spitfire that proved so successful during the Second World War.

OPPOSITE TOP: The floating bridge operated between the hard at the foot of Bridge Road in Woolston and Crosshouse at Southampton from 1838 until 1977, when the Itchen Bridge opened. The floating bridge carried cars, bicycles and foot passengers and saved a long journey across the River Itchen via Northam or Cobden Bridges. This 1960s card shows the old Supermarine building in the background.

SERVICE with **EFFICIENCY**

A.A.

R.A.C.

LARGE and WELL EQUIPPED GARAGE ACCOMMODATION

FULLY TRAINED and EXPERIENCED STAFF

- Complete OVERHAULS (Mechanical and Electrical)
- Cylinder Reboring on the Spot (by most up-to-date process)
- Battery Repairs
- Power Washing and Cleaning

VAUXHALL, FIAT, MORRIS, STANDARD, CARS

Satisfaction GUARANTEED

111 Commercial Road

HILLMAN, HUDSON, TERRAPLANE CARS

Large Car Park

Close to Central Station and Empire Theatre

Telegrams Auto.

Munn & Underwood Limited of Southampton.

Telephone 5001 & 2

66

QUEEN MARY
LIVERPOOL

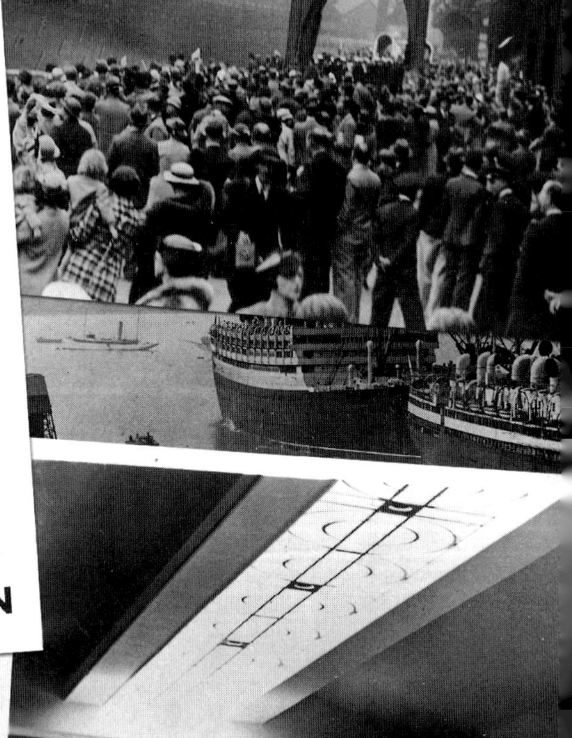

A

S.20511.
OCEAN TERM

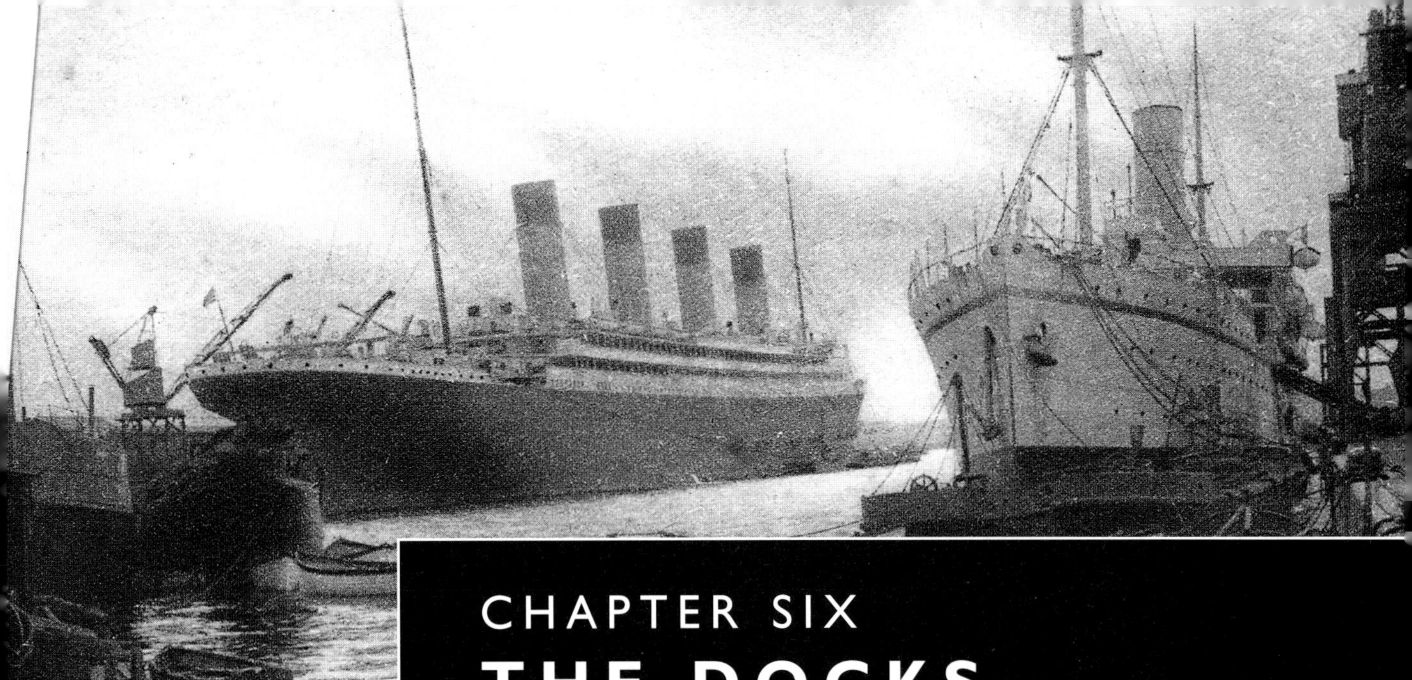

CHAPTER SIX
THE DOCKS

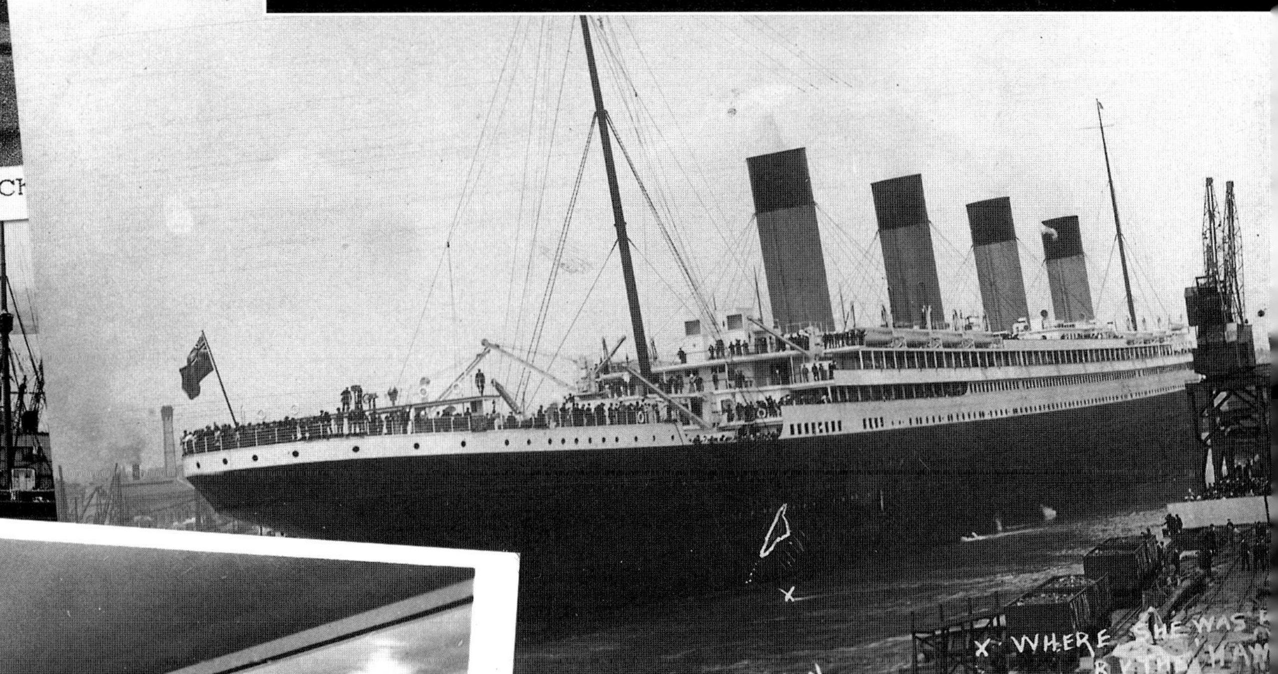

TOP: In the 1890s, when this photograph of the inner docks was taken, sailing ships were still dominant. Within a few years sail would be almost extinct as steamers began their reign of supremacy.

ABOVE: Opened in 1842, the Docks rapidly expanded and this 1890s photograph shows P&O's *Arcadia* preparing to berth in the open dock. Note the masts of a sailing ship in the drydock and the coal barges waiting to 'coal' a waiting ship. In the foreground on the left is a paddlesteamer.

TOP: The Empress Dock with a Union Castle liner on the right, circa 1920.

ABOVE: An American Line *SS New York* advertising card. She was built in 1888 as the *City of New York* for Inman Lines and was renamed when she was sold to the American Line in 1893. With a capacity of 725 steerage, 250 second class and 290 first class passengers she had a long working life. She was finally broken up in 1923.

TOP: The view of Southampton from the Docks in 1907. The Town Quay is in the foreground with the jetty to the pier just behind. The two spires of Holyrood and St Michael's Churches can be seen in the distance.

ABOVE: The Trafalgar Graving Dock was the largest dry dock in the world when it was opened in 1905. The dock was 912 feet long and had the capacity to hold 100,000 tons of water. When filled, it could be emptied again in just four hours.

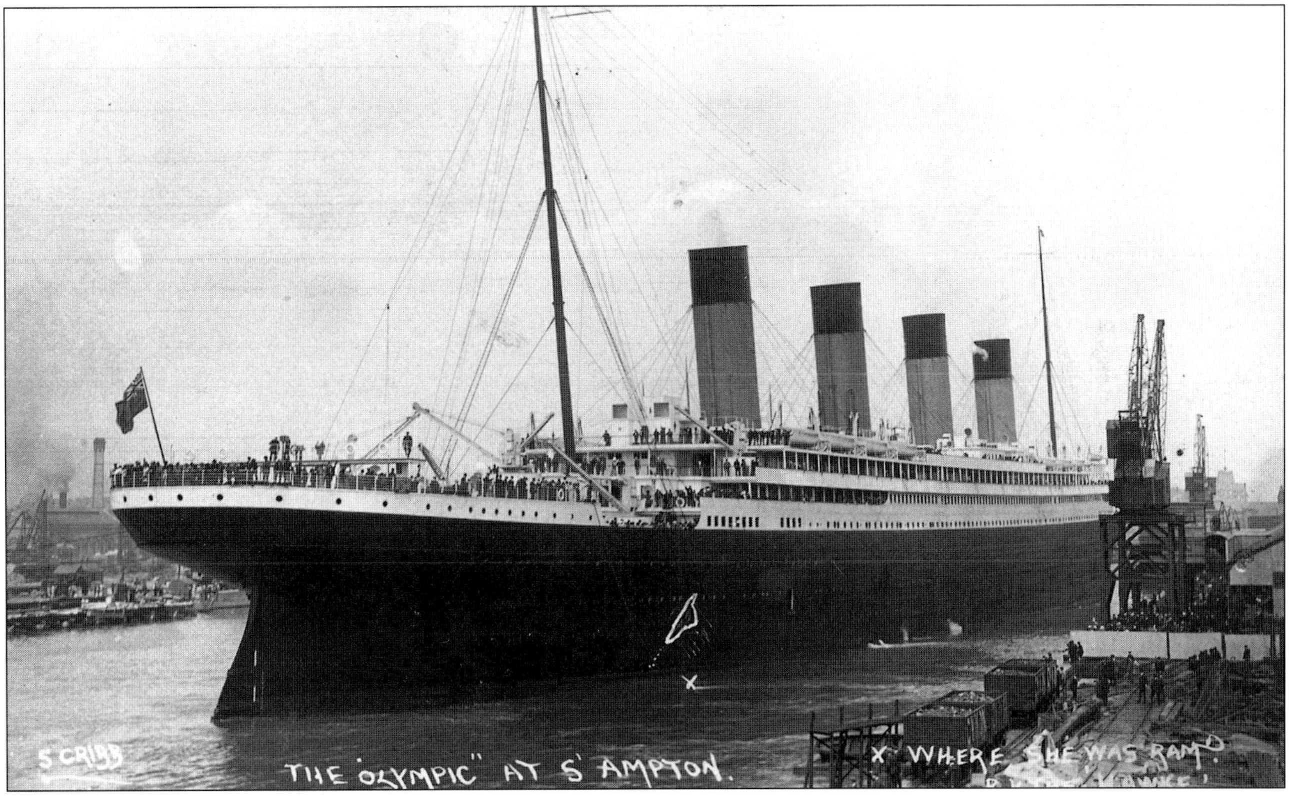

TOP: *SS Deutschland* in the Trafalgar Dry Dock. Built in 1900 for Hamburg-America Line, she was 16,502 tons and could carry 2,050 passengers. In 1911 she was renamed *Victoria Luise* and in 1921 she became *Hansa*. In 1925 she was broken up.

ABOVE: *SS Olympic*, the sister ship to *RMS Titanic* at Southampton following her collision with *HMS Hawke* off the Isle of Wight in 1911. When the two ships collided, the ram on the bow of the cruiser caused the damage (indicated in white on the photograph). The *Olympic* disembarked her passengers in Southampton before returning to Harland and Wolff's shipyard in Belfast for repair. Her arrival in Belfast meant work on the new liner *Titanic* was delayed. *Titanic's* maiden voyage had been scheduled for March 1912, but she finally embarked on April 10. But for the twist of fate involving *Hawke* and *Olympic*, perhaps *Titanic* would have been just another liner with Southampton as her home port.

TOP: The White Star or Ocean Dock with *SS Olympic* tied up at the same berth from which *Titanic* sailed. The lifeboats in the foreground are being checked for seaworthiness.

ABOVE: Interior of the White Star office in Canute Road. Originally built in 1893 for the American Line, from 1907-1931 White Star Line also shared this office. Some of the passengers aboard the *Titanic* would have purchased their tickets at the counter in the foreground. Outside the building, families of crew members of the *Titanic* gathered to wait for news or to read the names of survivors posted on the noticeboard.

TOP: The White Star Dock with Cunard's *Mauretania* and *Aquitania* on the right and the *Olympic* and an American Line ship on the left. Opened in 1911, this huge dock became Ocean Dock in 1922.

TOP: The White Star liner *Suevic* ran aground on the Lizard in 1907. The ship was cut in half and while the bow was left on the rocks, the stern was towed to Southampton. The white crosses indicate where the ship was severed in two.

ABOVE: This picture shows the damaged part of the stern of the *Suevic* when she arrived in Southampton. A new bow was built by Harland and Wolff's Belfast shipyard and towed to Southampton where the ship was reassembled.

TOP: Built by Armstrong Whitworth of Newcastle, this floating dry dock was opened by HRH the Prince of Wales in 1924. Moored near the Town Quay, it could hold ships as large as 60,000 tons. When the huge King George V dry dock was opened in 1933, it was no longer required and became redundant.

ABOVE: An aerial photograph taken in November 1929 shows the construction of the New Docks and the reclamation of the land at Western Shore. In the centre of the photograph are the first quays for the New Docks. At the bottom in the centre, the Royal Pier can be seen along with the reclaimed land for Mayflower Park.

ABOVE: On October 15, 1938, the Chairman and Directors of the Southern Railway Company held a celebratory supper for their supervisors and clerical staff at Southampton Docks to mark the Southampton Docks centenary. Although the foundation stone for the Docks was laid in 1838, they were not completed and opened until 1842.

TOP: *RMS Queen Mary's* maiden entrance into Southampton in May 1936. She is steaming past the *Majestic* and the *Arundel Castle* on her way to King George V Dry Dock. At 81,000 tons, she was the largest liner in the world.

ABOVE: The departure of *RMS Queen Mary* on her maiden voyage to New York on May 27, 1936. More than 150,000 people gathered to watch her sail and when she arrived in New York so many wanted to greet her that the city ground to a halt. In August 1936 she took the Blue Riband, for the fastest Atlantic crossing from her rival the French liner *Normandie*. She was sold to the City of Long Beach in 1967 and is now a museum, hotel and conference centre.

ABOVE: This 1960s shot shows the *Queen Mary* at the Ocean Terminal. In the background is the second *Mauretania*. The Ocean Terminal had its own railway station for passengers travelling by liner. The rounded end of the Ocean Terminal building housed offices and a port control area.

TOP: The art deco style Ocean Terminal was opened in 1951. Originally designed in the 1930s, the building had very high specifications with fine woods from around the British Empire. This photograph is of the lounge filled with leather couches and a W H Smith & Son bookstall in the centre.

ABOVE: A closer view of the bookstall. Built primarily for 'the Queens', this splendid arrivals and departures building was unfortunately demolished in 1983.

OPPOSITE: The visit of *USS Forrestal* to Southampton in 1957 was quite an experience for the town. The largest warship to call at the port, she was open for public viewing and an estimated 65,000 eager visitors toured the ship, with thousands more being turned away due to lack of time. Some local children had their first experience of American ice-cream during their visit on board. The people of the town gave the crew a fond welcome with many being invited into the homes of local families.

The Fifty-Niner

Vol. 3 No. 16 — USS FORRESTAL (CVA-59) — October 21, 1957

ENGLAND PROVES TO BE HOST OF HOSTS OFFERS FORRESTAL UNRIVALED WELCOME

THE USS FORRESTAL, escorted by tugboats, moves slowly up the River Test at dusk on Sept 30th. The Cunard Luxury Liner, Queen Elizabeth, is in the background as the carrier approaches her berth at Piers 108 and 109 in Southampton, England.

He giveth His beloved sleep

CHAPTER SEVEN
THE TITANIC

TOP: *RMS Titanic* en route to Southampton on April 2, 1912. After trials in Belfast Lough, she steamed to Southampton arriving at midnight on April 3. She stayed in the docks for a week while provisioning took place. To ensure all aboard would not go hungry or thirsty, 75,000lbs of fresh meat, 40 tons of potatoes and 40,000 fresh eggs, together with 20,000 bottles of beer, 1,500 bottles of wine and 850 bottles of spirits, were stored below decks. She carried a wide range of cargo from a passenger's Renault car right down to velvet, ostrich feathers and hair nets.

ABOVE: This photograph was taken on April 10, the *Titanic* had just set sail from berth 43 and was passing what is now the *QEII* terminal. At 46,000 tons she was the largest ship in the world. On the night of April 14, she collided with an iceberg with the loss of 1,500 passengers and crew; 549 of the crew lost were from Southampton.

TOP: The *Titanic* passing the *SS Oceanic* at Dock Head having nearly collided with the *New York*. Suction from the passing *Titanic* caused ropes that were mooring the *New York* to break. The liner swung out into the path of *Titanic* which would have resulted in serious damage. The fine seamanship of crew members averted a collision.

ABOVE: Passing Dock Head with the liners *Oceanic* and *New York* in the background.

TOP: Approaching Hythe pier and just about to let go her tugs.

ABOVE: There are very few photographs taken on board *Titanic* and none were taken of her grander rooms. As the interiors of the sister ships *Titanic* and *Olympic* were almost identical, this photograph of the *Olympic's* first class smoking room gives a very good indication of the style and opulence that the first class passengers enjoyed. However, first class ladies were not permitted in this room, which was said to have taken on the atmosphere of a gentlemen's club. The picture above the fireplace is by Norman Wilkinson and can be seen in Southampton's Maritime Museum. The picture that hung above this fireplace on the *Titanic* was also by the same artist.

TOP: *RMS Titanic* was fitted out with great attention to fine workmanship and all the facilities possible for the comfort of her passengers. While walking on deck and playing deck games have always been popular with passengers, the *Titanic* was very modern, as she had not only a swimming pool but a gymnasium. The gym had a range of equipment including exercise bicycles, rowing machines and a mechanical horse. In attendance was Mr McCawley whose role was to ensure that passengers received instruction and encouragement should they wish to take some strenuous physical exercise.

ABOVE: Relatives and friends of missing crew members gather outside the offices of the White Star Line in Canute Road, Southampton on April 17, 1912 to read the names on the noticeboard. The lists were altered as more information became available. At times mis-spelling of names caused distress and confusion.

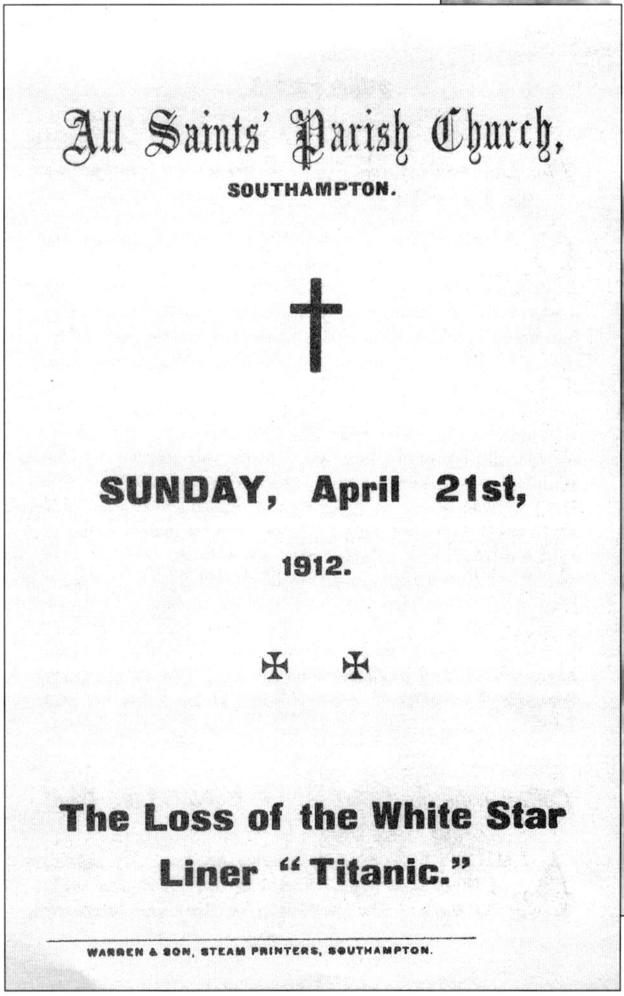

All Saints' Parish Church,

SOUTHAMPTON.

✝

SUNDAY, April 21st,

1912.

✠ ✠

The Loss of the White Star Liner "Titanic."

WARREN & SON, STEAM PRINTERS, SOUTHAMPTON.

TOP: A 2001 photograph of the same White Star Line building shown on page 123. Built in 1893, it was used by White Star Line from 1907-1931. After recent renovation, the building is once again used as offices.

ABOVE LEFT: On Sunday April 21, memorial services were held in towns and cities across the country. The congregation of All Saints Parish Church in High Street offered prayers for those who were lost and those who suffered in the tragedy.

ABOVE: It was unusual for both a brother and a sister to be crew members on board a ship. This is a photograph of Violet McClaren nee Allsop of Shirley Road who was one of the stewardesses that was saved. Her brother, Richard, who was also a steward, was unfortunately lost. He lived at 73 Obelisk Road, Woolston.

These two photographs (ABOVE and TOP) are of the officers and crew of the White Star Line marching to St Mary's Church for a memorial service on April 21. *(Photographs courtesy of Southampton Maritime Museum.)*

TO THE MEMORY OF THE ENGINEER OFFICERS
OF THE R.M.S. "TITANIC" WHO SHOWED
THEIR HIGH CONCEPTION OF DUTY AND THEIR
HEROISM BY REMAINING AT THEIR POSTS
15TH APRIL 1912
ERECTED BY THEIR FELLOW ENGINEERS AND FRIENDS
THROUGHOUT THE WORLD.

Now the labourer's task is o'er;
Now the battle day is past,
Now upon the farther shore
Lands the voyager at last.
FATHER, in Thy gracious keeping
Leave we now Thy servant sleeping.

G. T. YOUNG, PRINTER, SOUTHAMPTON.

In Loving Memory of

FREDERICK TAMLYN,

The beloved Son of

ALFRED AND ANNIE TAMLYN.

Who lost his life at Sea through the
foundering of the S.S. TITANIC,
April 15th, 1912.

Aged 23 Years.

ABOVE: A memorial card for Frederick Tamlyn who lived at 20 Southampton Street. Frederick, aged 23, joined the *Titanic* as a mess steward. His body was recovered and he is buried in Halifax, Nova Scotia.

RIGHT: A memorial to the firemen and crew of the *Titanic* was unveiled on the Common in 1915. Because of vandalism, the memorial was relocated in 1972 and is now in Holy Rood Church Merchant Navy Memorial.

OPPOSITE: A memorial to *Titanic's* engineers was unveiled by Sir Archibald Denis in 1914. This striking memorial remembers the engineers' devotion to duty, which resulted in the electric light being maintained for as long as possible, enabling others to escape from below decks. No engineers survived.

PLUMMERS
uthampton
Information
2d-
AUGUST
The Month's
FILMS
&
Entertainments
TRAIN
SERVICES
LOCAL
Information
PUBLIC
AIR RAID
SHELTERS
Full List
CINEMA PROGRAMMES
SPORTS
DANCES
ENTS OF THE MONTH
HAT TO SEE
TRAVEL SERVICES
LOCAL
INFORMATION
SOUTHAMPTON'S OWN PRIVATE CAR HIRE SERVICE
PHONE
5151
For Immediate Service
SOTAX
DAY OR NIGHT
C&A

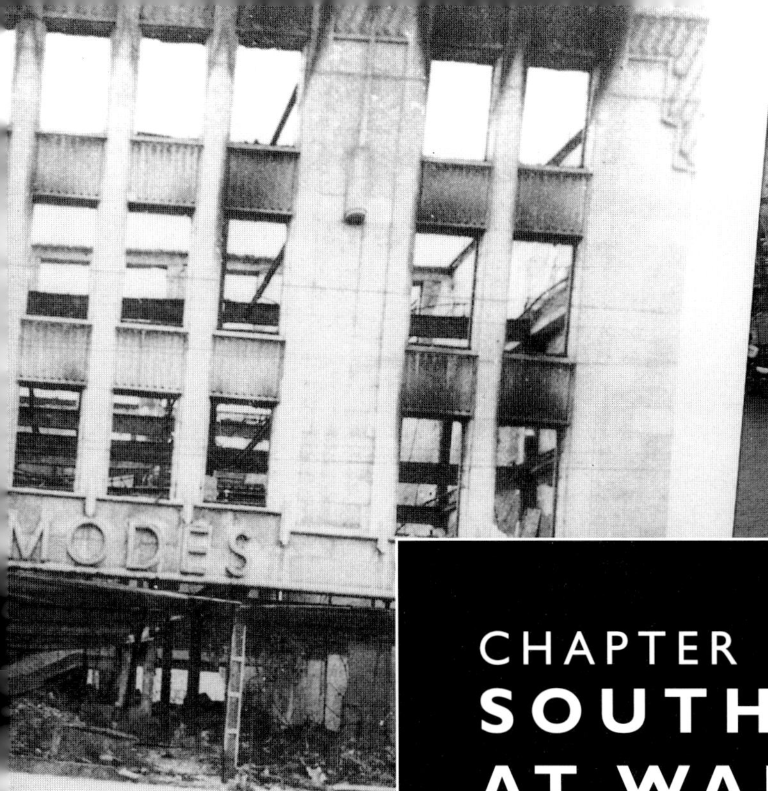

CHAPTER EIGHT
SOUTHAMPTON AT WAR

TOP: On November 25, 1940, the town came under attack in a daylight bombing raid. A bomb fell through the roof of the Art Gallery and there was also extensive damage to other parts of the Civic Centre including the Art School block where fourteen schoolgirls – members of a party from the District School – were killed.

ABOVE LEFT: The view through the damaged dial of the Civic Centre clock showing the bomb crater in the courtyard between the municipal block, Guildhall and the Law Courts. The bomb, which was estimated at 2,000lbs, caused considerable damage and left a crater 60ft wide and 15ft deep.

ABOVE: The stone guardians that stood at the entrance to the Art Gallery. One was totally destroyed and the other was removed during re-building. The caption on the photograph proclaims: '...bloody but unbow'd...'

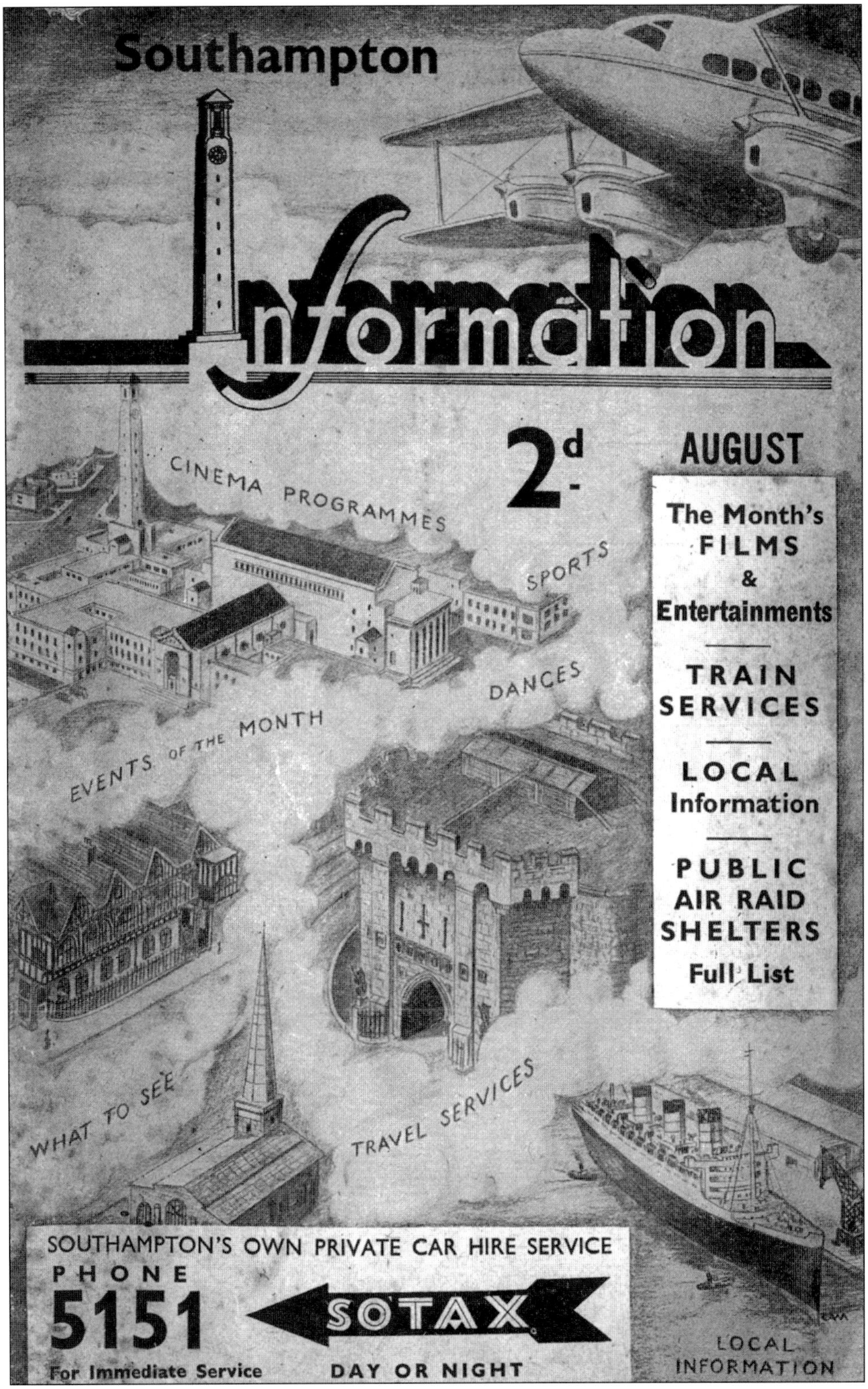

ABOVE: An Information booklet for August 1940. This handy edition provided information about sport, entertainment, trains and ferries. There were fourteen cinemas around the city which advertised very varied programmes and features were usually changed twice weekly. The Forum in Above Bar was showing Spencer Tracey and Robert Young in *Northwest Passage* while the Empire in Commercial Road ran Arthur Askey in *Charley's Aunt*. Those living in the suburbs need not travel into town as there were several local cinemas. In Portswood the Palladium was showing *Geronimo* while the main feature at the Savoy in Swaythling was Judy Garland in *The Wizard of Oz*. The booklet also provided important information about the location of public air raid shelters.

C&A MODES
C&A
C&A

PLUMMERS

OPPOSITE TOP: The burnt-out shell of C&A Modes in Above Bar Street after the heavy bombing raids of November and December 1940. Over a period of two weeks the bombers attempted to destroy the town centre and inflicted heavy casualties. C&A was re-built and traded in the same location until it closed in 2001.

OPPOSITE BOTTOM: Further along Above Bar was Plummers department store which also suffered severe damage. They continued to trade in small shops around the town until re-building in the 1950s. This popular store closed in the 1990s. The building was taken over by Southampton Institute and after modernisation was re-named the Sir James Matthews building.

TOP: All that remained of a Southern Railway's store in the docks which was destroyed by fire during the 1940 blitz.

ABOVE: The Highfield Company of the Home Guard proudly pose for their photograph on August 29, 1940.

ABOVE: The blast from this explosion has sent a carpet flying into the air, finally becoming caught on overhead tram lines.

TOP: This photograph taken in November 1942 is of an army logistics exercise which involved loading equipment into ships at the quayside.

ABOVE: October 1944 and a Southern Railways train gets ready to disembark German prisoners-of-war who can be seen in the secure compound in the centre of the photograph. They were housed in a temporary holding camp near Dock Gate 8.

Miss. E. H. Davidson.

COM: SOUTHTON

County of Southampton.

As Lord Lieutenant of the County I desire to express my thanks for, and to place on record my appreciation of, the services given by you as Duty Officer, Report Centre. from 24.10.42 to 2.5.45 in Civil Defence.

I view with pride and satisfaction the contribution to the successful prosecution of the war made by the Service to which you belong, and I send you this individual token of my gratitude for your work.

Mottistone

The Castle,
Winchester.

Lord Lieutenant
of Hampshire.

CIVIL DEFENCE

OPPOSITE: A Civil Defence certificate awarded to Miss Davidson, who served as a duty officer in the Report Centre from 1942 until 1945.

TOP: *RMS Queen Elizabeth* in war paint with her decks crowded with troops as she berths at the Ocean Docks in 1945. The quayside is lined with thousands of well-wishers waiting to greet the returning troops.

ABOVE: *RMS Queen Mary* in her war colours approaching 106/7 berths in the New Docks in 1945. Winston Churchill believed that the ability of the two 'Queens' to carry up to 15,000 troops in every Atlantic crossing had shortened the war by two years. Both ships resumed passenger service following fitting-out at the end of the war.

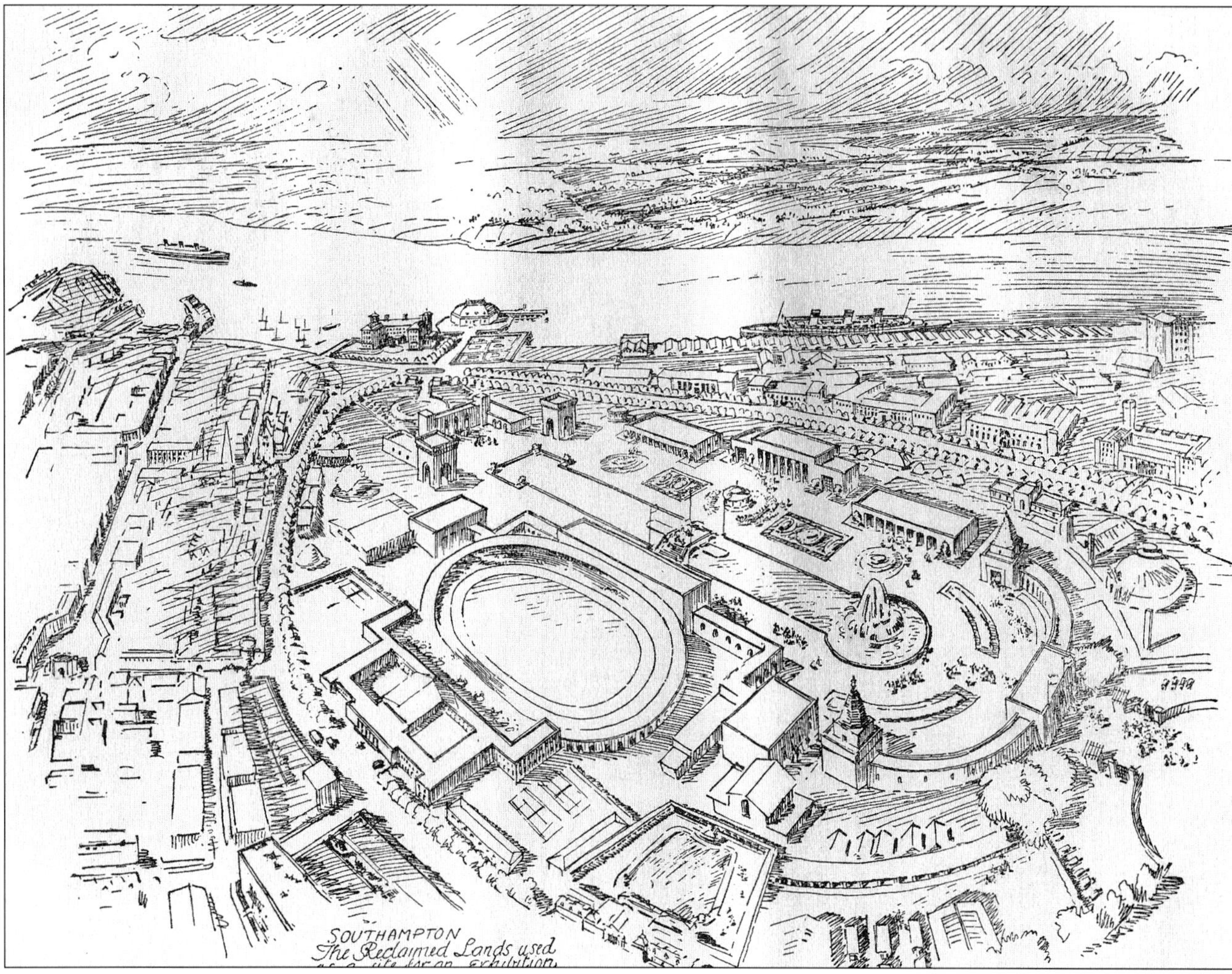

ABOVE: In 1942, in preparation for peace-time, the town planners issued a classified report entitled *The Replanning of Southampton* which outlined the suggested re-design and re-building of much of the town centre that had suffered at the hands of the Luftwaffe. These plans show an uncluttered town centre with imposing buildings and the addition of new parks. In the centre of the town, opposite the Civic Centre, an imposing 'circus' would be an important architectural feature of the plan. Measuring 500ft in diameter with a promenade of shops at first floor level behind a row of columns, the shops would be undercover and would provide shelter for shoppers as they walked around the circus. On the re-claimed land where the new West Quay development now stands, were plans for an open recreation area with a youth centre, stadium and open-air baths. It was also thought to be the ideal site for exhibitions. This diagram shows the lay-out for the reclaimed land with the Royal Pier in the distance and the Bargate on the left.

OPPOSITE TOP: Winter of 1945. Heavy snow blankets the ruins of shops and offices as a tram makes its way along High Street. Re-building of High Street continued until the end of the 1950s.

OPPOSITE BELOW: Heavily damaged during war-time bombing of the town centre, Edwin Jones' department store (now Debenhams), underwent a re-building programme in the early 1950s. This photograph shows reconstruction of the Queensway store is well underway

NOW REBUILDING EDWIN JONES
SOUTHAMPTONS LARGEST STORE

St. Lukes
V

CHAPTER NINE

AROUND SOUTHAMPTON

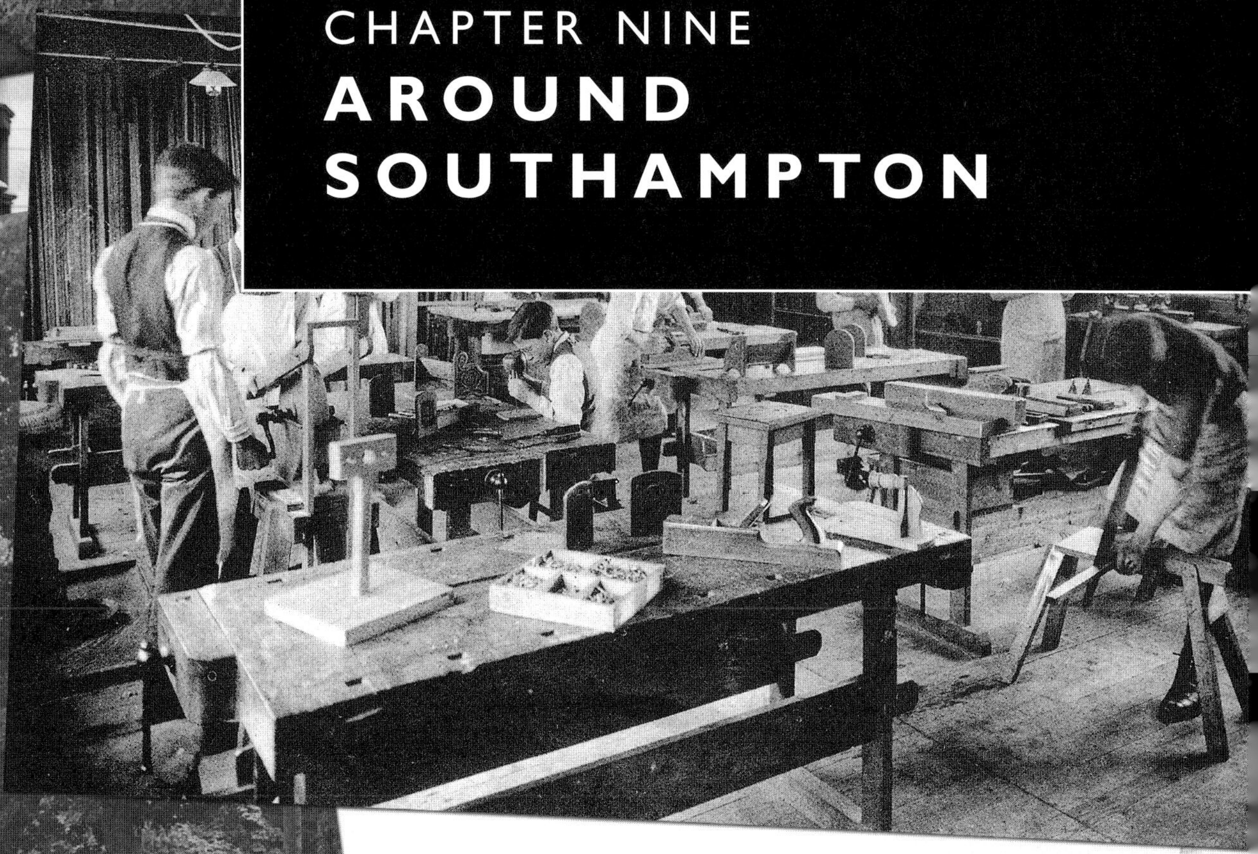

TOP: The Stag Gates that stood at the junction of Lodge Road and The Avenue in 1905. Erected in 1844 as the entrance to Bevois Mount House, they were taken down for road-widening in 1919. While some of the stonework was re-used in East Park, it is believed that the stags were buried in the grounds of Bridell Lodge in Regents Park Road in 1920 by the auctioneer and estate agent William Burrough Hill.

ABOVE: The appearance of the Cowherds Inn on the Common, here pictured in 1902, has changed little in 100 years. It was originally built as an inn in 1762. It takes its name from the cowherd who was employed by the town to look after the townspeople's cattle on the Common.

ABOVE: The Infirmary at Shirley Warren. Built in 1900, this small hospital grew rapidly into the important regional teaching hospital that Southampton General Hospital is today.

TOP: The village of old Shirley in 1902. On the right is the Blacksmiths Arms on Romsey Road.

ABOVE: High Street, Shirley, in 1910. The High Street was, and still is, the main shopping area for Shirley residents. On the right hand side one can just make out part of the White Hart Hotel. Further along, William Gange and Sons the boot manufacturers on the corner of Church Street are advertising American shoes for sale. On the opposite side of the road is England's the ironmongers, with a large selection of goods hanging outside the shop to tempt customers.

TOP: Looking in the opposite direction along Shirley High Street at the junction with Church Street in the 1960s. International Stores now trade from the building once owned by Gange's shoes. On the other corner is J Baker and Co, the men's outfitters and next door is Kyle's shoe shop.

ABOVE: The elegantly tree-lined Shirley Avenue in 1910 looks much the same as it does today.

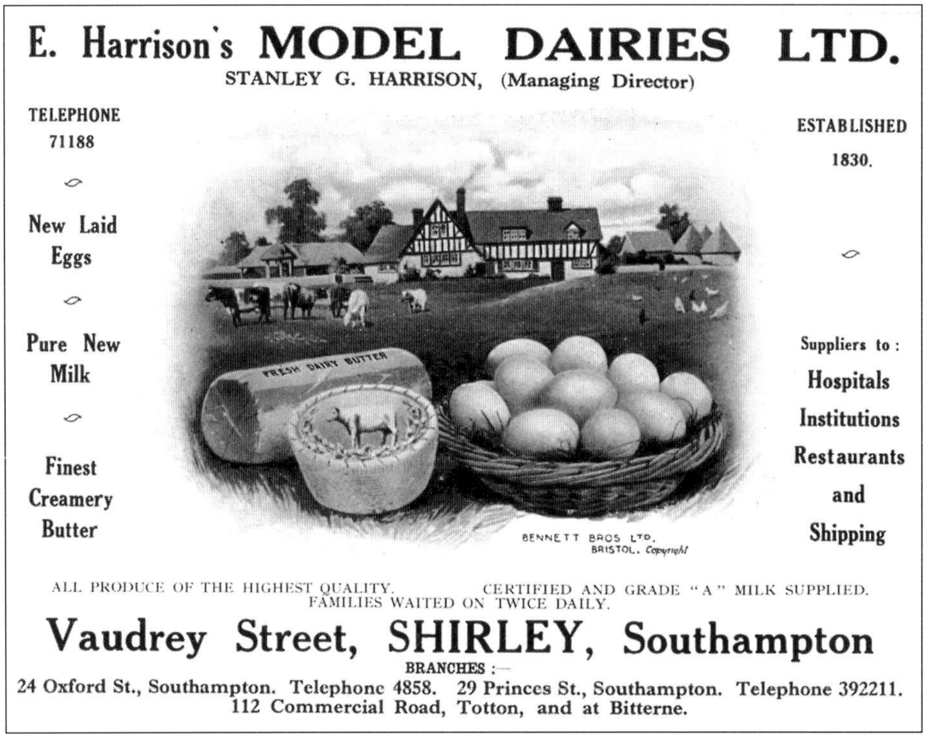

ABOVE: The Vicarage of Christ Church in Highfield Lane.

TOP: Highfield Church (Christ Church) at the junction of Church Lane and Highfield Lane.

ABOVE: South Stoneham House, the residence of Lord Swaythling was also called The Grange. This card shows a rear view of the house and gardens in 1910. The house, situated at the junction of Mansbridge Road and Wide Lane, was demolished in the 1960s.

OPPOSITE: A photograph of the fountain in the gardens at The Grange in 1918.

TOP: Swaythling Railway Station before 1914. Built in 1883 for London and South Western Railways, the station also had a goods siding alongside. As many as twenty trains called at the station daily and travelling into the town centre by train was very popular with local residents.

ABOVE: The first Cobden Bridge spanning the River Itchen between St Denys and the new suburb of Bitterne Park was opened in 1883. The toll-free iron bridge was named after the Liberal reformer Richard Cobden and was demolished in 1926. This 1904 view of the bridge is from St Denys looking towards Bitterne Park.

Bitterne Park Estate,

SOUTHAMPTON.

COBDEN BRIDGE.

Particulars

WITH

PLAN AND CONDITIONS OF SALE,

BY AUCTION, ~~ON THE ESTATE,~~

AT

THE "ROYAL HOTEL," SOUTHAMPTON,

On TUESDAY, 24th APRIL, 1894,

At 2.30 p.m.

A. W. PEARCE, Esq.,
Solicitor,
21, JOHN STREET, ADELPHI,
LONDON, W.C.

F. G. WHEATLEY,
Auctioneer and Land Agent,
CLEMENT'S INN CHAMBERS,
263, STRAND, LONDON, W.C.

ABOVE: The second and current bridge was built between 1926 and 1928. This photograph shows the newly-completed bridge viewed from Bitterne Park looking towards St Denys. Today the bridge is still one of the few places to cross the river from the east side of the city and is one of Southampton's busiest roads.

LEFT: Particulars of the auction of building land at Bitterne Park Estate in 1894. The sale was held at the Royal Hotel and included 93 freehold plots of land suitable for 'good villa residences' and cottages in Manor Farm Road, Oak Tree Road, Ash Tree Road, Cobden Avenue and the 'very pretty sylvan road known as Middenbury Lane'. A corner plot in Cobden Avenue together with a corner plot in Oaktree Road sold for a total of £212 10s 0d (£212.50).

TOP: Bitterne Park Triangle in the early part of the 20th century. Unlike today, there is little traffic and children played freely. The Woolston company Lankester and Crook Ltd were grocers, provision and wine and spirit merchants, with their head office in Obelisk Road. The Bitterne Park branch of Lankester and Crook's general store is on the right and they traded from this site until the 1980s. The shops, apart from changing hands, look much the same today.

ABOVE: A more recent photograph of the same corner in the 1950s. Next door to Lankester and Crook's store on the corner is the National Westminster Bank, now an antiques centre. Opposite is the clock tower which was originally situated at the junction of Above Bar Street and New Road which was moved to this site in 1934.

ABOVE: Bitterne village in 1905. The junction of Bitterne Road and Bursledon Road with the Red Lion at the apex. While the two roads still remain important routes in and out of Southampton, the Red Lion sits today at the head of a thriving shopping precinct.

TOP: The Red Lion Cut, Bitterne, circa 1920. The 'cut' was a small lane running at the rear of the Red Lion. There were a few terraced houses and a shop. At the end of the cut is the Congregational Church which was later demolished to make way for the by-pass.

ABOVE: Situated almost opposite the Red Lion is the Church of the Holy Saviour, built in 1853. This interior shot was taken in 1904.

TOP: Physical training at Itchen Secondary School. The building was heated by a coal-burning stove which can be seen on the right. This hall was burnt down in December 1930.

ABOVE: The handicraft room at Itchen Secondary School. While the boys were instructed in wood and metalwork, the girls perfected their cooking and needlework skills.

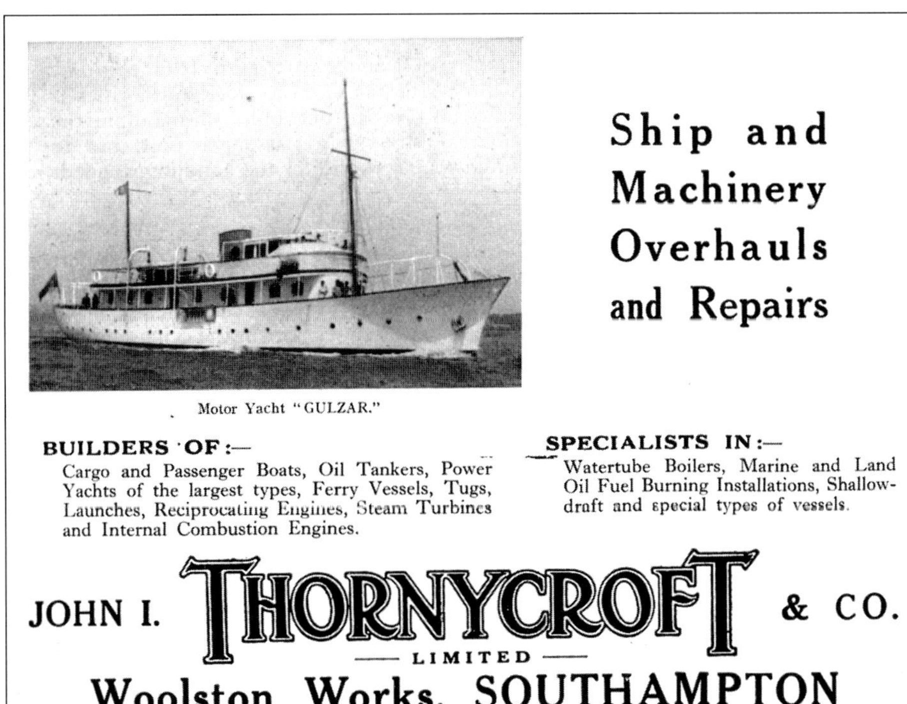

TOP: Victoria Road, Woolston, circa 1916. On the right is J Pell the chemist and further along, just past a temporary corrugated-iron building, is a branch of the Southampton Co-operative Society.

J. G. BOYES & Co.

C. PARNELL – PROPRIETOR

WOOLSTON - - SOUTHAMPTON

HOTELS
RESTAURANTS
ETC.
SPECIALLY
CATERED
FOR

CONTRACTORS
TO THE
LEADING
STEAMSHIP
COMPANIES

DAILY
DELIVERIES
BY
MOTOR
LAUNCHES
TO YACHTS
IN
SOUTHAMPTON
WATER

PROMPT
ATTENTION
DAY AND
NIGHT

YACHTING and SHIPPING BUTCHERS and GENERAL PROVISIONERS

TELEPHONE: SOUTHAMPTON 88570 TELEGRAMS: BOYES & CO., WOOLSTON

TOP: The view from the opposite side of Victoria Road in the 1960s. Vosper Thorneycroft's shipyard can be seen in the background.

TOP: Portsmouth Road, Woolston, viewed from the floating bridge circa 1916. In the centre is the Woolston Picture House that opened in 1913. Also known by the unsavoury name the 'Bug Hutch', it operated as a cinema until 1973. After refurbishment, the building became a bingo hall and continues to pull in the crowds today.

ABOVE: St Luke's Church in Onslow Road, Bevois Valley, during the heavy snowstorm that blanketed the south of England in 1908. The snow was so deep that trams could not run and travel became almost impossible as all forms of transport ground to a halt. St Luke's was erected in 1853 and was enlarged by the addition of a chancel and organ chamber over the next thirty years. The main thoroughfare through Bevois Valley was busy and thriving with shops and businesses lining both sides of the road.

Echo
SOUTHERN NEWSPAPERS
PUBLISHERS'
SOUTHERN DAILY ECHO HAMPSHIRE ADVERTISER
DRAMATIC TURN IN SECOND TEST
SMALL ADS. BRING BIG RESULTS.

THE END